THE LOCAL CHURCH
IN A GLOBAL ERA

THE LOCAL CHURCH
IN A GLOBAL ERA

Reflections for a New Century

Edited By

Max L. Stackhouse
Tim Dearborn
Scott Paeth

WILLIAM B. EERDMANS PUBLISHING COMPANY
GRAND RAPIDS, MICHIGAN / CAMBRIDGE, U.K.

© 2000 Wm. B. Eerdmans Publishing Co.
255 Jefferson Ave. S.E., Grand Rapids, Michigan 49503 /
P.O. Box 163, Cambridge CB3 9PU U.K.

Printed in the United States of America

05 04 03 02 01 00   7 6 5 4 3 2 1

Library of Congress Cataloging-in-Publication Data

The local church in a global era: reflections for a new century \
edited by Max L. Stackhouse, Tim Dearborn, Scott Paeth.
p.   cm.
Includes bibliographical references.
ISBN 0-8028-4710-2 (pbk. : alk. paper)
1. Church renewal. 2. Church renewal — United States.
3. Church and social problems. 4. Evangelicalism.
5. Christianity — Forecasting.
I. Stackhouse, Max L. II. Dearborn, Tim. III. Paeth, Scott.

BV600.2 L68 2000
250 — dc21   00-032151

www.eerdmans.com

Contents

CONTENTS

II. FAITH, LEARNING, AND FAMILY

III. THE SPIRIT, WHOLENESS, AND HEALTH

IV. CHRIST, THE CHURCH, AND OTHER RELIGIONS

Contents

Foreword

The U.S. church has long been known for its compassion for the poor, its concern for the downtrodden, and its global involvement. Our participation with government on issues of foreign aid, human rights, trade, and environmental protection policies is of vital importance. Our advocacy and active leadership within our churches and denominations for more expansive and integrated global engagement is needed now more than ever. And how we choose to lead our lives continues to be an important example to our children and neighbors as we begin a new millennium, a *global millennium*.

Together, the whole of society — including churches, academia, mission agencies, NGOs, government, civil society, and community groups — needs to seek new strategies for a more comprehensive global engagement that has a positive impact on all God's creation. These strategies must empower the poor as well as the rich, the oppressed as well as the favored, the marginalized as well as the powerful. This can only be done through individuals like you and me who are willing to be the voice for the voiceless. Speaking of the successes of the civil rights movement, Andrew Young said: "These changes all evolved through the actions of people — people of faith who courageously responded to the conflict, chaos, violence, and hatred around them with a mysterious but magnificent faith."

Brian Sellers-Petersen

Preface

The editors would like to thank all those who put their hard work, their intellectual energy, and their Christian spirit into this volume. As Max Stackhouse points out in his introduction, a great deal of work was done — in a very short time — by all of those involved. We have been gratified by the willing, indeed joyful, cooperation of World Vision, Princeton Theological Seminary, Eerdmans, and the contributors to both the book and the video portions of this project.

A word on how we anticipate our readers might use this book: The Media Services office of Princeton Theological Seminary has edited a video for use by churches and other groups in conjunction with this book. It includes commentary by several of the contributors as well as others who took part in the October 1998 conference at Princeton Seminary. We encourage you to use this book along with the videotape, which we hope will be used to open sessions, encourage further discussion, provide additional perspectives, and deepen the views presented in this volume. For this purpose, the book and videotape are available for purchase together.

Our hope is that, as a result of the book and accompanying video, churches, study groups, campus ministries, and other organizations may come to see the importance of globalization for the future of the Christian faith. How we respond to the ethical and spiritual challenges toward which we are moving will determine the character of our faith into the next millennium. May God's grace allow us the foresight and the courage to enter these challenges prayerfully.

Tim Dearborn
Scott Paeth

An Introduction

In some ways it was an odd marriage. But it worked. It proved that contrary bits of folk wisdom sometimes both apply: "Birds of a feather flock together" and "Opposites attract." World Vision (WV) is a nondenominational, relatively young, West Coast, largely Evangelical partnership of Christians which has become the largest Christian development and relief organization in the world. They asked Presbyterian, East Coast, largely Ecumenical Princeton Theological Seminary (PTS), one of the oldest academic centers in America for the training of clergy and teachers, to co-host a conference and to aid in the publication of materials intended to help redefine missions for the next century. The Pew Charitable Trusts blessed this liaison with a grant to cover some of the costs.

PTS and WV invited some one hundred leaders in the analysis of world trends, government, law, business, area specialists where global changes are dramatic, theologians, social ethicists, and leaders of church-related service, relief, development, and mission organizations from Evangelical, Ecumenical, Roman Catholic, and Eastern Orthodox branches of the Christian tradition as well as from some non-church related service and advocacy organizations. We met in the fall of 1998. We worshiped, discussed, debated, and ate together. Respondents and critics evoked modulation or revisions of perspective and sometimes sharp rejoinders. The editors worked their magic on selected presentations in the summer of 1999. Eerdmans is publishing the results; the Media Center edited the video.

1

This book and the related audio and video tapes, the first fruits of this agreeable marriage of convenience, are the primary public results intended for use in local churches.[1] What bonds these groups and the chapters of this book together is a commitment to carry out a faithful and useful ministry and mission under the new conditions of "globalization." The conversion of persons, the planting of churches, the care for those struck by disaster, and the building up of educational and medical institutions will continue to be priorities for many mission-oriented bodies, although much of this is increasingly carried out around the world by indigenous churches now growing stronger in numbers, independence, and resources. Nearly all of those invited to our conference have had extensive cross-cultural experience and know very well that church and mission bodies outside the "North" and the "West" are developing their own theologies and strategies for ministry, mission, and service. Some of the perspectives and programs are, in fact, sharply critical of "Northern" or "Western" influences. We also had to recognize the fact that "globalization" is widely viewed with suspicion, for it appears to be another "North" and "West" development that is intruding into their societies, cultures, and churches. Being fully alert to these critiques, we felt it was time to think through, again, how we ought to respond to them under the new conditions we face, build partnerships with promising developments in ways that also serve the needy, promote justice, cultivate the prospects for peace, and contribute in faithful ways to what seems to be the formation of a new global society that will undoubtedly include those committed to other religious traditions.

Surely it is true that the Christian churches face a new global situation, full of both promise and peril. Led by new developments in economics, technology, and media, by wider and more direct contact between the world religions, and by a wider consensus about human

---

1. The conference was coordinated with another smaller collection of scholars with international backgrounds who are studying these issues on an ongoing basis at the Center of Theological Inquiry. They not only joined in and contributed to this World Vision/Princeton Seminary event, but are continuing their research into issues raised by (or related to) the questions discussed in this book. Four volumes, primarily intended to help professors in university departments of religion and seminaries think through the issues posed by our new situation, entitled *God and Globalization*, will appear between 2000 and 2002 from Trinity Press International.

rights, ecological dangers, and the costs of war, new institutional and social practices are emerging on all sides. These contribute to an awareness of global interconnectedness and interdependence. However, new forces of fragmentation and domination are also made possible by just these developments. Several reports indicated that the very globalization that draws the world into a cosmopolitan civilization is experienced by many as a disrupting intrusion that they can neither fully resist nor warmly embrace. Following an image suggested by John Mbiti, the noted scholar of African Religions, some called it "the bulldozer effect."

How shall we think of the mission of the church in such a world? What needs modification? What can be modified? Many of the habits of mind that have stamped church policies, missionary practices, and service programs during this last century were fostered not only by profound religious convictions but also by (usually unintended) cultural imperialism and social domination. This was sometimes reinforced by no small amount of anxiety in the face of secularization and the simultaneous rebirth of "New Age" religions (which seemed to be "Old Age" paganism to many). Further, the experience of two World Wars, the Cold War, the wars of liberation, and new waves of ethnic, interreligious, tribal, or nationalist violence that seem to break out on every continent suggests that the rough places of human history have not yet been made plain. Some of the habits of mind and mission policies infected by these developments, and some of the habits and policies born of protest against them, are now obsolete and even debilitating. The churches cannot constructively undertake important changes without a better understanding of the emerging situation, a rethinking of what we have to offer to this kind of a world, and how best to offer it.

The central concern of these essays is the relation of Christian theology and ethics to key areas of global change. New levels of interconnectedness and interdependence can be found in many areas of life, and it is a deepening of faith to see how widely the implications of Christian thought reaches. Many topics that are likely to influence the future deeply are seldom discussed in churches, although they already have begun to affect the lives of believers at home and abroad. When they are discussed by Christians they are not always related to issues of faith or ethics. In the conference and in this book, they are treated from a Christian theological point of view. No one wants to turn congregations into a university course on world development, and no one expects every pastor to become an expert in all these areas. But if the churches are to develop effective missions in the next century, some of these matters are unavoidable.[2]

It is impossible to summarize here all the contributions made or topics taken up at the conference. Ongoing research is needed in several areas. Some topics seemed more indirectly related to congregational church life, and a few of the materials that were presented have been or will be published elsewhere by the authors. (Audio tapes of all presentations are available from the Educational Media Center of Princeton Theological Seminary.) However, we have selected five clusters of issues that pastors and congregations will find critical as they too think through the mission of the churches in our time.

1. Stewardship, Doing Well, and Doing Good

It would be foolish to try to deal with globalization without reference to the economy. Whether it is viewed as the triumph of capitalism, the spread of the market logic, the commodification of the earth, or the materialistic victory of consumerism, it is the economy that often first comes to mind when people hear the word "globalization."

Although traders have plied their wares by backpack, caravans, and waterways for as long as there is recorded history, most people lived by hunting, fishing, herding, or farming; all were essentially extraction methods in particular places. Commercial activities were centered in the inherited crafts, supplying those who lived by extraction or were connected to the more luxurious lives of political leaders.

A series of developments historically related to Christianity generated a distinctive "work ethic" as a sign of obedience to God. It began in

2. However, the Association of Theological Schools, which accredits the seminaries and divinity schools in North America has recently established a requirement that all its members, to remain in good standing, must develop programs that deal with globalization. Future pastors, priests, and local churches will be the beneficiaries. The entire issue of the journal *Theological Education* (Spring 1999) is dedicated to the issues, experiences, understandings, and challenges that globalization brings to the faculties who train clergy.

the monasteries where the life of disciplined work was integrated into a life of disciplined prayer, and later became applied to the "priesthood of all believers." Also, the church generated a set of institutions independent of kinship or regime that were to evolve into "the modern corporation," the primary workplace for more and more people who now work in factories, stores, or offices linked to the global economy. From its roots in medieval church law where "corporation" had to do with the rights of religious communities to own property in common, provide services, produce goods, and trade as a body different from the household and the body politic, it gradually shed its "religious order" roots and grew to become the host institution for the industrial revolution and for international trade — as we know not only from old factories, but from the old European companies for trade, banking, and finance.[3]

This new kind of institution was able to operate on a wider basis, over a longer period of time, and with greater economic effectiveness than any economic institution built around the household or managed as a branch of government. It grew in influence over the last few centuries, especially in America, although it was sharply opposed in the twentieth century by various forms of socialism in the name of the workers, and by a number of forms of fascism in the name of national sovereignty. It became the home of technological innovation, and in the process altered ideas of property, work, job, and profession. It brought about changes in family, political, and cultural life.

After the defeat of fascism and the failure of Soviet socialism, corporate influence has exploded across all borders and traditional boundaries, drawing more and more of the world's population and more aspects of social life into a common web of corporate relationships. What we call the "market economy" is increasingly shaped by these relationships. Various large corporations and international banks have made loans to developing countries which have sometimes aided development, sometimes been diverted into the private accounts of political leaders, and sometimes become the occasion for crippling debt repayments if development did not take place well enough to establish a flourishing economy.

3. See my "The Moral Roots of the Corporation," *Theology and Public Policy* 5, no. 1 (1993): 29-39.

There are a number of benefits to the new corporate economy. Most evidence suggests that people are best off where there are higher numbers of corporations per population, and most leaders of poor countries or regions want to get corporations to put up their factories and offices there. Very few want to return to socialism or fascism or to remain in perpetual underdevelopment. Still, many see globalization essentially as a boundless corporate capitalism which may outproduce other systems, but which also demands frenetic work schedules, increased materialism, and the marginalization of all those not in on it. Where corporations encounter traditional economies, attitudes, and patterns of relationship, it introduces a crisis — people want its products, but resist its demands and hate its disruptive effects on social life as they have known it. It appears that mammon has found a new home from which to rule the world. How does spirituality relate to this kind of organization? Can the church and the faith contribute anything to the salvation of a world now shaped by this powerful reality?

It is neither prudent nor possible to leave these matters entirely in the hands of secular specialists. Many of the issues needing attention have moral and spiritual dimensions. Many people who are involved in the churches are also involved in business, labor, transportation, technology, and administration, or are simply interested in the wider church and world affairs. They know that many of the issues we face have been influenced by and have implications for people beyond their own congregation and nation, and are laden with moral and spiritual overtones. However, there is only scattered evidence of moral or spiritual approaches to the critical issues. Indeed, many suggest that it is a time of fragmentation, breakdown, and pending chaos precisely because no moral and spiritual foundations can be found by these means.

Those who spoke to these issues in the conference were realistic about problems, but they remain convinced that the faith provides resources that are now needed. When the authors of these chapters take up one or another area to clarify what is happening around the world, they also seek to discern what God is doing in the midst of these changes and to chart practical new directions for ministries and missions as we move into the twenty-first century.

In the first set of essays, Professor William Schweiker, a United Methodist theologian from the Divinity School of the University of Chicago, The Right Reverend James H. Ottley, bishop of the Episcopal Church, and Dr. David Befus of World Vision, take us into some of the most critical issues we presently face, religiously and practically, regarding economic globalization. (See the comments on their contributions on pp. 23-25.) They show that through responsible stewardship as taught in the Bible and in the classic theological tradition, the effects of mammon can be constrained. Indeed, they show how some aspects of economic globalization can be rechanneled to help those who are now doing badly do well, and they show how the missionary impulse in every believer can lead us to do some economic good in and for the world.

2. Faith, Learning, and Just Loving

Globalization is not only economic. We shall see in later parts of this book that technology, ecology, the encounter with other faiths, international law, and the perils of war are also global influences. But globalization is not only about things that have happened or do happen or could happen high above and far away from where most people live. It is a feature of globalization that what happens "out there somewhere" has an impact on what happens here — in our schools, homes, and churches. It is called "reflexivity"; what happens there reflects back on here and what happens here reflects back on what happens there. This is one of the key reasons for holding this conference and preparing this material. Local communities need to be prepared for what is happening, and to decide whether to resist or embrace it. Also, the long-range cumulative effect of what people do in local communities will influence the direction and destiny of globalization. This part of the book helps us recognize global reflexivity in Christian education, marriage, and worship.

The church, the family, and the school are central to any viable and enduring civil society. They shape personal conviction. Character is formed, love is nurtured, and understanding is cultivated in them. If people are to be prepared morally, emotionally, and intellectually to shape the global future, and not to be swallowed or devastated by it, they must be equipped to face the global environment in which they will live. That requires an informed mind, a capacity for principled commitment, and a profound faith. Yet, in some ways, the school, the family, and the

7

church often find themselves besieged by influences and forces they do not quite know how to face.

In America, the separation of church and state (for which there are very good theological as well as practical political reasons) has meant that many grow up without knowing much about the religious traditions that have shaped Western civilization generally and the social and political life of the United States in particular. Often, young people know a great deal about neither what the other religions of the world have to offer nor how religion works in other cultures. For that reason, new efforts at Christian education are underway. Some of those engaged in leading these new efforts have recognized that the complex issues of globalization need to be introduced as a dimension of Christian education.

Christianity is a missionary religion, and we need to understand the nature and character of our mission, especially under new conditions. Further, in our public schools, faith is very often presented as but one aspect of culture, with the implied notion that every culture and every religion is equally valid. This may aid tolerance, but it may more often breed insecurity, doubt, and an unwillingness to make deep and informed commitments. Still further, the mobility and migrations of people in our day mean that more people in more communities face one or another kind of pluralism and multiculturalism simply by meeting others in the families of friends, in the neighborhood, at school, and at work. How shall we teach the next generation to cope with the inevitable multiculturalism of the global future without losing faith?

Ideas of pluralism and multiculturalism appear in every area of life. Plural forms of family life and marriage have been much discussed in the last several decades. Issues of divorce, remarriage, blended families, single-parent and same-sex families are hotly debated in many churches. The rise of feminist consciousness, which is partly tied to the changing patterns of work outside the home, and partly to new understandings of justice in the relationships of men and women, has also had a profound effect on the shape of family life in the West, and it is having increasing impact around the world. Indeed, it is now possible to speak of "global feminism" as a movement. Increased exposure to the role of family and faith in other traditions is reshaping our own understandings of marriage and family life in general, sometimes helping to correct efforts to reform family life in ways unlikely to stand the test of time or to nurture a healthy and faithful next generation.

Similarly, we can say that worship is today influenced by plural and multicultural exposure. Missionaries were among the first to report to the Western churches about religious similarities and differences. Many of the early anthropologists were sons and daughters of missionaries. But as the church was planted in many places, the new churches began to selectively adopt and to actively alter what they received. Thus, they began to become full partners in the development of the ongoing Christian traditions, just as Greeks, Romans, Northern Europeans, Slavs, etc., had done historically. An indication of this can be found in the worship resources that are now widely used. Nearly all denominations have revised their hymnal in the last generation, and they have all included materials from around the world. Worship is altered by this reflexivity. This is not the place to reprint international hymns, but it is a good place to illustrate how sermons and meditations written by someone from another culture can deepen our own worship.

Thus, the second set of essays is focused on school, family, and church — all under the title of *Faith, Learning, and Family*. It includes contributions by United Presbyterian Richard Osmer, a professor of Christian education at Princeton Theological Seminary, the Christian Reformed feminist scholar, Dr. Mary Stewart Van Leeuwen, lay church leader and professor at Eastern College, and worship meditations by Fr. John Mbiti, already mentioned above as one of the world's leading scholars of African Religions, an Anglican priest from Kenya now serving in Switzerland. (See further comments on their contributions, pp. 61-62.)

3. The Spirit, Wholeness, and Health

Economic life, plus the reflexive influence of educational, family, and worship life, shape globalization and are shaped by it. The same goes for technology. While it was once thought that science changed the world, it now appears that technology, using science, changes it more radically and is developing more rapidly. Clearly, it is a globalizing force and like others, is laden with promise and peril. In the past such technical innovations as the use of fire, harness, the iron plow, gunpowder, sextant, clock, and printing had worldwide effects, but seemingly over a long period of time. Faithful people could morally and spiritually digest their implications and extend implications of the first principles embedded in biblical and theological perspectives to guide them. But it is not clear that we have done so well with the internal combustion engine, the splitting of the atom, or the host of newer technologies that alter both the internal structure of human existence and the fundamental structure of the environment.

It has been argued that Christianity is heavily responsible for Western technological change, for we have been given the mandate to "have dominion" over the earth and all that is therein. Further, later theological developments argued that because both humans and nature are fallen, it is the duty of believers to use "the mechanical arts" to restore what can be restored, to improve what can be bettered, and to oppose the powers of death and disease.[4] Such arguments indicate that parts of the Christian tradition have been very much related to issues of technology and saw it, rightly used, as a spiritual and moral instrument. Certainly, missionaries over the centuries have been agents of technological transfer wherever they went. Today the connection between moral, theological, and spiritual insights and the technologies shaping globalization is less direct and more difficult to define.

Three areas are especially challenging. First are the biotechnical interventions that change the genetic codes of the human person. Second are the ecologically invasive economic interventions that are changing the biophysical environment. And third are the medical technologies that make interventions possible at the boundaries of life and death.

Striking contributions to the discussion of these issues can be found in Ron Cole-Turner's essay. He is a professor of theology at Pittsburgh Theological Seminary and editor of one of the first books published on cloning. Susan Power Bratton, who has written on ecological issues from a theological perspective, offers an intriguing case study in "econormative" thinking about one critical issue confronting our oceans. And Dr. Allen Verhey, a noted medical ethicist, takes up the explicit

---

4. A current fascinating treatment of these themes can be found in David F. Nobel, *The Religion of Technology: The Divinity of Man and the Spirit of Technical Change* (New York: A. Knopf, 1998).

question of the relationship of the Holy Spirit to contemporary understandings of medicine. We gain fresh insight from them into the state of
contemporary technology as a global force and ways to think about it in
terms of *The Spirit, Wholeness, and Health.* (See the comments on these
contributions on pp. 97-99.)

4. Christ and Other Religions

The impact of economics, of reflexivity in Christian education, family
life, and worship, and of technology influences also the global encounter
with other religions and other branches of Christianity. The world religions are no longer "long ago and far away"; they are present in our
communities. The rich philosophies of India and of China, especially
Hinduism and Confucianism — both extremely complex with many
variations — have long proven that they could shape great pluralistic
cultures over many centuries. Moral ideals and social patterns adopted
from them have made a major impact on the surrounding cultures of
their regions. But they are also increasingly present in other societies
due to the migration of Indian and Chinese peoples into nearly every
country of the world. Something similar could be said about primal religions — tribal and shaman traditions which in times past covered huge
areas of the globe and which today persist in the ways that Christianity
is practiced in many places when these people are converted.

Historically, missionaries to India and China and tribal regions
have been intrigued and perplexed, if sometimes affronted, by the practices of these traditions, and ritual forms of meditation, exercise, and
dance have been adopted by non-Hindus, non-Confucians, and non-
tribals in many places. Those who came to know the intellectual, spiritual, and moral philosophies behind them often found areas of possible
agreement or convergence. Besides, for the most part, neither Hinduism
nor Confucianism nor the tribal religions are missionary religions; they
do not emphasize conversion or doctrine. One is born and nurtured into
these traditions. One learns its practices as one becomes a part of the
society. Ethnicity, faith, geography, and social practice are deeply inter-
twined into a kind of cultural genetic code.

Something of this is surely true of all great religions, but Buddhism,

11

Islam, and the various branches of Christianity are also missionary and doctrinal religions. They seek to have people understand their message as carried in their faith's doctrines, to see its truth, and to convert. In this regard, they are in principle, if not always in fact, more concerned about expressed belief than ethnicity or cultural practice as the marker of faith. They all also seek to convert the whole world, so that they reach beyond any geographic or national boundary. And while they link faith and social life, they seek to do so in ways that subordinate the conventions of society to the principles of faith.

Of course, the various branches of Christianity find areas of common ground with each other and with these great world religions, and all stress tolerance at certain levels. Finally, though, on certain matters of doctrine they simply do not agree, and each would like to convert the others. For this reason, interfaith relationships with Buddhists and Muslims and ecumenical relationships among Protestant, Catholic, and Orthodox Christians, and between, say, Pentecostal and Liberationist branches of Protestantism and Catholicism, have sometimes been conflictual. Looked at another way, however, some aspects of Buddhism appear to have parallels with the more liberal parts of Christianity, while Islam seems to have parallels with the more conservative parts of Christianity, as these essays show.

A decisive issue for the global future is how these religions are going to understand one another and relate to each other. Our contributors to this part of the volume bring intriguing backgrounds to these questions. Kosuke Koyama, professor of world Christianity Emeritus of Union Theological Seminary in New York, was born and raised in Japan, where he was converted to Christianity. Later, he became a missionary to Thailand and became, in a new way, acquainted with Buddhism and an interpreter of that tradition to Christians as well as an interpreter of Christianity to Buddhists. Lamin Sanneh, professor of missions at Yale Divinity School, was born into a leading Muslim family in West Africa, and converted to Christianity, first to Methodism and more recently to Roman Catholicism, as he pursued his intellectual and spiritual journey. Working with a number of ecumenical and interfaith bodies, he became a key interpreter of Islam to Christians and Christianity to Muslims and an innovative interpreter of the missionary process in general.

We end this portion of the book with an essay by Cecil M. Robeck, Jr., an evangelical professor of missions at Fuller Theological Seminary. One of the leading Roman Catholic scholars of missions and globalization, Fr. Robert Schreiter, has written a widely quoted book on "the new catholicity."[5] Although he was unable to come to the conference to dialogue with Professor Robeck, something of the flavor of dialogue is captured in Robeck's essay on "the new ecumenism" that concludes this section. (For further comments on these contributions, see pp. 139-41.)

5. Conflict, Violence, and Mission

The issues of conflict in the global situation must be faced by a genuinely catholic, genuinely evangelical, and genuinely ecumenical spirit. It is unlikely that all conflict and violence will be eliminated from human history, for it is one of the deepest truths of the Christian tradition that sin plagues our personal and social lives from beginning to end. One might even suggest that the ancient pagan god Mars continues to lurk under the mantle of civilization and is constantly threatening to break free. But it is also part of the theological and ethical mission of Christians to reduce conflict and constrain violence. The means to do that take us into areas that also have been deeply shaped by Christian history in the past, but which now seem to operate without overt connection to the faith or the church. I refer specifically to law and politics.

It is one of the most difficult features of globalization that it has no legal or political boundaries or government. Living in a constitutional democracy, we know that when a civil liberty is challenged we can say "it's a free country." And when something dangerous is at hand, we can say "there ought to be a law." In either case, we can appeal to the legally guaranteed rights to preserve our freedoms or to mobilize an action committee, advocacy group, or political movement to get a new law passed. Historically, the formation of our constitutional democracy was deeply stamped by Christian influences and shaped by profound ideas of just law and compassionate mercy.

But in the global society into which we are moving, no constitution

5. Robert Schreiter, *The New Catholicity: Theology Between the Global and the Local* (Maryknoll, NY: Orbis Books, 1997).

governs and no democratic institutions are in place. It is true that more international law has been passed in the last quarter of a century than in any century previously, indicating that some, albeit vague, notions of justice are in play; and it is true that more countries have adopted democratic constitutions during that period than ever before in history. But a certain anarchy continues to exist in international relationships. The United Nations, of course, has become effective in some areas of international cooperation, and its "Universal Declaration of Human Rights" is a marvelous achievement to which many aspire; but it seems unlikely and probably not desirable to have the UN develop into a single world government. How then can and should we respond to the sporadic violence and conflict that pops up now and again in every corner of the globe? What is the Christian mission in such a situation?

John Witte, Jr., director of the Law and Religion Program at the Law School of Emory University, has coordinated a series of scholarly and practical programs dealing with interfaith and cross-cultural perspectives on human rights and democracy. With the help of Gary Haugen of the International Justice Mission, who did on-the-ground investigations of the conflicts in Rwanda for the UN, Witte presented us with an overview of the factors that lead to and potentially help contain interreligious conflict. We begin this section with it.

Donald W. Shriver, Jr., until recently president of Union Theological Seminary and a past president of the Society of Christian Ethics, has written and lectured widely on the problem of reconciliation between hostile groups and nations. He explicitly treats the distinctive contribution that Christians can make in this area. And we conclude this section, and the book, with an essay by Ian T. Douglas, a professor of theology and Missions at Episcopal Divinity School, who reviews not only these specific issues, but many of the themes touched on in the entire volume, and brings the implications back to the possibilities and responsibilities for mission in the local church. (For further comment on these contributions, see pp. 179-81.)

*   *   *

Such a volume as this could not have been written without the cooperation of many. We are indebted especially to the editors of this volume, who, along with Kelley D. Reese of Princeton Theological Seminary, and Steve Commins and Brian Sellers-Petersen of World Vision, worked collegially and efficiently with me on the planning committee. Brian Sellers-Petersen worked closely with Joicy Becker-Richards of the Media Center and her staff at PTS to edit the audio and videotapes. Margaret Paeth also provided invaluable assistance by proofreading the final manuscript. We were supported throughout by President Thomas Gillespie and Vice-President Adrian Backus of PTS, and by outgoing President of WV, Robert Seiple, and his successor, Richard Stearns. Both institutions generously supported the event. The Project on Public Theology at PTS and the Institute for Global Engagement at WV supplied all the early funding for planning and coordination, and the Pew Charitable Trusts made the grant that made the entire project and publication finally viable, as already mentioned. Finally, we want to thank those besides the authors and those mentioned here who attended and contributed so much to the conversations and discussions, and to the ongoing research in these areas. They are listed on the following pages.

Max L. Stackhouse
Princeton Theological Seminary

Adetokunbo Adelekan
Princeton Theological Seminary
Princeton, NJ

Ann Alexander
Rutgers University
New Brunswick, NJ

Nancy Ammerman
Center for Social and Religious
  Research
Hartford Theological Foundation
Hartford, CT

Jesudas Athyal
M. M. Thomas Foundation
Madras, India

Vincent Bacote
Drew University
Madison, NJ

Craig Barnes
National Presbyterian Church
Washington, DC

David Befus
World Vision
San Jose, Costa Rica

Dale Hanson Bourke
Religion News Service
Washington, DC

Susan Power Bratton
Whitworth College
Spokane, WA

Elizabeth Brookens-Sturman
First Presbyterian Church
Bethlehem, PA

Frederic Burnham
Trinity Institute
Trinity Parish
New York, NY

James Callaway, Jr.
Trinity Grants Program
Trinity Parish
New York, NY

Tom Chabolla
Roman Catholic Archdiocese of
  Los Angeles
Los Angeles, CA

John Clause
World Vision
New York, NY

Ron Cole-Turner
Pittsburgh Theological Seminary
Pittsburgh, PA

Steve Commins
The World Bank
Washington, DC

Stephen Crocco
Princeton Theological Seminary
Princeton, NJ

An Introduction

Kenda Creasy Dean
Princeton Theological Seminary
Princeton, NJ

Tim Dearborn
Seattle Pacific University
Seattle, WA

Thomas Derr
Smith College
Northhampton, MA

David Devlin-Foltz
Aspen Institute
Washington, DC

Ian Douglas
Episcopal Divinity School
Cambridge, MA

Abigail Evans
Princeton Theological Seminary
Princeton, NJ

Gerald Flood
United States Catholic
   Conference
Washington, DC

Charles B. Ford
InterVarsity Christian Fellowship
Madison, WI

Francis Fukuyama
George Mason University
Fairfax, VA

Anthony Gaeta
The World Bank
Washington, DC

Fe Garcia
World Vision
Federal Way, WA

William P. George
Dominican University
River Forest, IL

William Getman
First Presbyterian Church
Woodstock, NJ

Thomas W. Gillespie
Princeton Theological Seminary
Princeton, NJ

Charles L. Glenn
Boston University
Boston, MA

Wesley Granberg-Michaelson
Reformed Church in America
New York, NY

Walter Grazer
United States Catholic
   Conference
Washington, DC

Stanley Green
Mennonite Board of Missions
Elkhart, IN

17

Stephen Haas
Prayer for the Persecuted Church
Denver, CO

Deirdre Hainsworth
Princeton Theological Seminary
Princeton, NJ

Donald Hammond
World Relief
Chicago, IL

Susan Billington Harper
The Pew Charitable Trusts
Philadelphia, PA

Gary Haugen
International Justice Mission
Washington, DC

David Heim
The Christian Century
Chicago, IL

Frances Hesselbein
The Peter Drucker Foundation for
    Nonprofit Management
New York, NY

Toby Huff
University of Massachusetts
North Dartmouth, MA

John Huffman
St. Andrew's Presbyterian Church
Newport Beach, CA

Gareth Icenogle
First Presbyterian Church
Bethlehem, PA

Shirley Jacobsen
First Presbyterian Church
Bethlehem, PA

James T. Johnson
Rutgers University
New Brunswick, NJ

Donna Katzin
Shared Interest
New York, NY

Garvester Kelly
Baptist Mission
Kinshasa, Democratic Republic
    of Congo

Leonid Kishkovsky
Orthodox Church in America
New York, NY

Barbara Kohnen
United States Catholic
    Conference
Washington, DC

Kosuke Koyama
Union Theological Seminary
New York, NY

David Krueger
Baldwin-Wallace College
Berea, OH

Steve Krentel
World Vision
Philadelphia, PA

Harold Kurtz
Presbyterian Frontier Fellowship
Portland, OR

Peter Kusmic
Gordon-Conwell Theological
    Seminary
South Hamilton, MA

David Landes
Harvard University
Boston, MA

Margaret Larom
Episcopal Church (U.S.A.)
New York, NY

Sang Hoon Lee
Princeton Theological Seminary
Princeton, NJ

Sang Hyun Lee
Princeton Theological Seminary
Princeton, NJ

Michael Livingston
Princeton Theological Seminary
Princeton, NJ

Gasper F. Lo Biondo, S.J.
Woodstock Theological Center
Georgetown University
Washington, DC

James Loder
Princeton Theological Seminary
Princeton, NJ

Randy Lovejoy
First Presbyterian Church
Florence, SC

David Mace
Northern Trust Global Advisors,
    Pacific Group
New York, NY

Mary Maxwell
Writer
Adelaide, Australia

Judith Mayotte
Seattle University
Seattle, WA

John Mbiti
Princeton Theological Seminary
Princeton, NJ

Marion McClure
Presbyterian Church (USA)
Louisville, KY

Paul McKaughan
Evangelical Foreign Mission
    Association
Atlanta, GA

Terry Muck
Austin Presbyterian Theological
Austin, TX

Ken Mulholland
Columbia College
Columbia, NC

James Nash
Center for Theology and
  Public Policy
Washington, DC

Robert Nelson
University of Maryland
College Park, MD

Ronald Nikkel
Prison Fellowship International
Washington, DC

Diane Obenchain
University of Beijing
Beijing, China

William O'Brien
Beesom Divinity School of
  Samford University
Birmingham, AL

Phil Olson
First Presbyterian Church
Mt. Holly, NJ

Dan O'Neill
Mercy Corps International
Portland, OR

Richard R. Osmer
Princeton Theological Seminary
Princeton, NJ

Bishop James Ottley
Anglican Observer to the
  United Nations
New York, NY

Scott Paeth
Princeton Theological Seminary
Princeton, NJ

Vincent Peters
Bethel College and
  Theological Seminary
St. Paul, MN

David Popenoe
Rutgers University
New Brunswick, NJ

Jennifer Pratt
Presbyterian Center for
  Mission Studies
Pasadena, CA

Kelly Reese
Princeton Theological Seminary
Princeton, NJ

Bob Rice
Association of Presbyterian
  Mission Pastors
Tulsa, OK

Cecil M. Robeck
Fuller Theological Seminary
Pasadena, CA

Roland Robertson
University of Pittsburgh
Pittsburgh, PA

David Robinson
World Vision
Lexington, MA

Shirley Roels
Calvin College
Grand Rapids, MI

Lamin Sanneh
Yale University
New Haven, CT

David Schmidt
Fairfield University
Fairfield, CT

Robert Schreiter
Catholic Theological Union
Chicago, IL

William Schweiker
University of Chicago
Chicago, IL

Chris Seiple
US Marine Corps
Washington, DC

Ambassador Robert Seiple
U.S. State Department
Washington, DC

Brian Sellers-Petersen
World Vision
Federal Way, WA

Donald Shriver
Union Theological Seminary
New York, New York

Ambassador Sheila Sisulu
South African Embassy
Washington, DC

Andy Smith, III
American Baptist Churches
Valley Forge, PA

Milan Sojwal
All Saints Episcopal Church
Princeton, NJ

Mark Southard
Presbyterian Frontier Fellowship
Bethlehem, PA

Max L. Stackhouse
Princeton Theological Seminary
Princeton, NJ

Richard Steams
World Vision
Federal Way, WA

Jay Steenhuysen
World Vision
Los Angeles, CA

AN INTRODUCTION

Mark L. Taylor
Princeton Theological Seminary
Princeton, NJ

John M. Templeton, Jr.
Physician
Philadelphia, PA

Thomas Thangaraj
Chandler School of Theology
Emory University
Atlanta, GA

Dennis Tornquist
Calvary Lighthouse
Lakewood, NJ

David Tracy
University of Chicago
Chicago, IL

Constantine Triantafilou
International Orthodox
  Christian Charities

Paul Tshihamba
First Presbyterian Church
Berkeley, CA

J. Wentzel Van Huyssteen
Princeton Theological Seminary
Princeton, NJ

Mary Stewart Van Leeuwen
Eastern College
St. Davids, PA

Rudolf Van Puymbroeck
The World Bank
Washington, DC

Alan Verhey
Hope College
Holland, MI

Miroslav Volf
Yale Divinity School
New Haven, CT

Donald Wagner
Center for Middle Eastern Studies
North Park College and Seminary
Chicago, IL

Sze-Kar Wan
Andover-Newton Theological
  School
Andover, MA

Kevin Wansor
Westminster Presbyterian Church
Wilmington, DE

Harry Winter, O.M.I
Oblate Center for Mission Studies
Washington, DC

John Witte
Emory University Law School
Atlanta, GA

Kathryn Wolford
Lutheran World Relief
Baltimore, MD

22

I

STEWARDSHIP, PROSPERITY, AND JUSTICE

Introduction

With the advent of the global economy, the slogan "think globally, act locally" has taken on a new importance. On the one hand, globalization has made the concerns of all the concern of each. We no longer have the luxury (if indeed we ever had it) of viewing the needs and wants of our own local community apart from the requirements of the entire world. From the shoes we wear and the food we eat to the companies for which we work, we are entwined with members of the human family half a planet away. On the other hand, these global concerns have implications for the way that we deal with those closest at hand. Globalization has changed, for better or for worse, some of the fundamental assumptions about our local responsibility for good stewardship, the creation and distribution of wealth, and the claims of justice.

When we turn our attention to the problems that attend the global economy, we shouldn't be surprised to find ourselves somewhat overwhelmed by the complexity we encounter. We haven't been trained to think very far beyond our own back door. Yet our Christian faith demands of us that our concern for our neighbor extend not only to our friends, but to the stranger, the resident alien, the foreigner. And globalization has brought the concerns of the stranger as close to home as those of our best friends and closest family members. But what resources does our faith offer us to respond to our new context?

23

The three essays in this section remind us of our Christian responsibility and help us to begin framing appropriate responses. William Schweiker sets forth the issues at stake in his essay, "The Church as an Academy of Justice." How, he asks, is it possible to be faithful to God in a world of mammon? Global capitalism has created a context in which all are in principle free to buy and sell, even themselves. Yet if this freedom reduces everything to a commodity, at what point do we lose our very humanity? As capital is no longer constrained by national borders, the world market will make it harder to maintain moral values over against monetary values. What kind of culture can we expect to emerge from this? What role ought Christians to play in such a situation? Schweiker argues that Christians have a responsibility to preserve a space in society in which persons may be respected in their very selves, without regard to the part they play in the global economy. As creatures of God, we have an innate dignity, which the demands of global capitalism must be bound to recognize.

The Right Reverend James Ottley, in his essay, "The Debt Crisis in Theological Perspective," looks at one element in the global economy from an Anglican point of view. Taking his lead from the 1998 Lambeth Conference resolution on world debt, he demonstrates how one religious body is attempting to lead the global economy to a greater recognition of the importance of maintaining human dignity in situations where it is in danger of being sacrificed. The Lambeth Conference did not set out to lay blame for the debt crisis, but rather sought to formulate an appropriate Christian response which recognized the legitimate requirements of both the indebted nations and their creditors. Additionally, it sought to recommend a new international mechanism for preventing a repeat of such crises in the future. Rooting his analysis in the "good news to the poor" preached by Jesus, Ottley calls on those in power to recognize the human dimension of the global economy and act for the good of the poorest of God's children.

Finally, David Befus provides an analysis of several strategies used by the churches to empower the poor to work for their own welfare in his essay, "Discovering a Role in God's Provision." Arguing for the necessity of sustainable development in poor nations, Befus gives examples of more and less successful approaches to this, asking which techniques worked and why. He considers the theological underpinnings of these approaches, and illustrates what vision of God and God's work inspires these strategies. He argues that Micro-Enterprise Development offers one very viable solution to the problems of sustainable development.

Taken together, these three articles provide an important analysis of the relationship between the global economy with which we are only beginning to come to grips and our responsibility as Christians. In a world of mammon, how do we maintain human dignity? How can a church body issue a prophetic call to compassion and solidarity? How can the poorest be helped to help themselves? The possibilities are manifold. These three essays provide a place to start this discussion.

Scott Paeth

1

The Church as an Academy of Justice: Moral Responsibility in the World of Mammon

WILLIAM SCHWEIKER

Justice and Persons

The 1900s marked the largest peacetime expansion of the U.S. economy in history. It also marked the expansion of international corporations as well as the globalization of commercial interests and images. The global economy, a $400 trillion-a-year giant, now creates whole new areas of business that reach beyond national laws and governments. Stock market crashes as well as the flow of capital and jobs around the world set new patterns of immigration and distribution of income. By some estimates roughly a fifth of the world's population lives in absolute poverty — fear, early death, squalid living conditions, disease. The fact of world poverty raises questions of justice in an age of wealth and scarcity. Scholars also speak of this period as the "decade of the economic pastorals" by Roman Catholic bishops and Protestant denominations. From the papacy to Wall Street there has been intense concern about and reflection on the moral, political, and economic features of global developments.

Paradoxically, human beings have developed economic systems that produce incredible wealth, yet endanger the worth and meaningfulness of their lives as moral agents. In response to this paradox, the church needs to see itself as an academy of justice, the place, that is, for the education and renewal of convictions about right relations. Christian convictions about justice are importantly related to beliefs about and evaluations of "the world." The church cannot and ought not simply exist for itself. It must seek to transform the world. Yet if we ask, as surely we must, about the meaning and value of the "world" in all of its complexity, it seems clear that for Christians meaning and value are always related to and dependent on agents who act in the world, create and shape reality, but are not ultimately reducible to the world. Nature and history have worth because God is creator; social systems and cultures are valuable because they are the work of human action.

At the heart of Christian convictions about justice is the calling to respect and enhance the integrity of life before God. That is why we care about the world, including the world of mammon. The trajectory of this essay, accordingly, is from clarifying beliefs about the world and current economic reality to presenting the claim that Christians, as disciples of Jesus, must continually learn, teach, and live the reign of God in human affairs. Stated simply, the task of the church is to be an academy of justice.

The World of Mammon

The very idea of "the world" is systematically complex in Christian faith. First, "world" is bound to the idea of creation as God's bestowal of being and worth. Creation is not a matter of exchange or refashioning pre-existent "stuff" on the model of labor. It is the gift of existence. Christian faith is radically monotheistic and this means creation is good. Next, the term "world" designates the realm of earthly reality; it is a descriptive term for the conditions of human life as orderly rather than chaotic. The ancients could speak of the "ecumenical" church, meaning thereby the whole civilized "world." Third, the "world" also denotes, in terms of conceptions of sin, that reality which does not know God or Christ and in fact opposes God's goodness and grace (cf. Jn 1:10). This is why Christians are to be "in" but not "of" the world. Indeed, one could gain the whole world and in doing so lose one's soul (Mk 8:36). The world of sin is a reality constituted by denial and destruction and yet driven, unknowingly, to continue its own undoing. Henceforth, in terms of salvation, the "world" is, fourth, that for which Christ suffered (cf. Jn 3:16). The depth of this conviction about Christ's saving work extends to the insistence that one can hope in God's glory and "a world without end." The idea of "world" is thus finally linked to eschatological convictions about the coming reign of God. This complex range of meanings of "world" implies that any proper Christian response to social and cultural existence will endorse its goodness as created, resist it as fallen, work for its transformation, and hope in its salvation.

Not unsurprisingly, this subtle account of the "world" is manifest in Christian responses to "mammon" and thinking about justice. The term "mammon" represents the Aramaic word for riches or wealth. It is probably derived from the Semitic root "mn" meaning "to be firm, reliable." Mammon is something secure; it is that on which one relies. In the New Testament it occurs only in the words of Jesus, but it is not uncommon in the Targums and Talmud. Throughout Scripture there is recognition of private property — for instance, the divine commands in the Decalogue against theft and the prescribed redistribution of wealth in the year of Jubilee. Divine blessing is often tied to prosperity and progeny, and, even in the parables of Jesus, the awareness that a worker is due his wages. Of course, within these parables the extravagance of the divine reign is presented in such a way as to overturn normal patterns of economic distribution. The least are given the most; the faithful son is not welcomed with the same abundance as the prodigal. Still, Scripture acknowledges the rightful place of "mammon" (wealth, gain, possession) in human life.

On the other hand, mammon has been seen as a basic threat to the moral and religious life. Given the linguistic root of the term, what is at issue is that on which persons rely, what provides security in life. Jesus repeatedly bids his followers to trust in God, not wealth, for the necessities of life. "You cannot serve God and mammon" (Mt 6:24 = Lk 16:13). Church fathers, like Tertullian and Chrysostom, wrote against the dangers of money. As early as Gregory of Nyssa, "mammon" was taken to be the name of the demon of riches or a Canaanite god. St. Augustine also noted that some things are to be used and others loved. Money is to be used, but only God is the fit object of ultimate love and enjoyment. Confusion at this level — where persons come to enjoy what ought only to be used — is sin, the confusing of what is not God for God. By the Middle Ages, and culminating in Milton's *Paradise Lost,* mammon was pictured as a demon. And in the Renaissance mammon was personified as greed, for example Sir Epicure Mammon, the greedy knight of Ben Jonson's *The Alchemist.* "Mammon" evokes fascination, grows into devotion, and can finally enslave persons.

For the classical Christian tradition in the West, "mammon" has been seen as a basic social "power." It is a sphere of life necessary for human existence, but tends to encompass the whole of life and in doing so displays demonic features. This is the root of the paradox that human beings can create systems of meaning that are self-negating. Economic activity and valuation must be set within, limited by, and judged according to more basic moral and religious norms. Not surprisingly, current work in Christian ethics focuses on the extent to which market societies are consistent with and can be made supportive of justice and the common good. Yet before turning to these matters, we must explore the "world of mammon" from another perspective. This will show us that cultural matters, and not just economic issues, must be addressed in the academy of justice.

Economic Globalization

Contemporary societies under the pressure of modernization and globalization are internally pluralistic. By "pluralistic" I mean that they are culturally diverse and socially differentiated. In these nations, diverse communities struggle for cultural recognition and viability. There is a seeming cacophony of voices among and within cultures. Additionally, different spheres or subsystems (economy, law, education, politics, media, etc.) work by their own logic, rules, norms, and primary purposes. In terms of economic life, the primary good is the creation of wealth in order to meet the economic needs of a society, namely, the needs of material well-being and survival. Pluralistic societies, if they function properly, require that the various subsystems interact and yet constrain each other. This is to ensure that no one subsystem gains a tyrannical relation to the social whole. "Commercialism," as opposed to commerce, is precisely that kind of situation: it is a social world in which there is no "outside" to commerce. Everything (labor, property, body parts) is commodified and salable. This would be the extreme, negative or sinful instance of the "world of mammon."

In a global context, these matters are even more complex. Human social "worlds" are constituted in part by economic activity. The global flow of cultural artifacts through commercial means — that is, the new "sign-value" of commodities beyond their manifest use and exchange value (e.g., Name Brand products; pictures of pop-stars) — shape human identities. We must therefore move beyond institutional analysis and examine the cultural question of how self-understanding and world-making are structured by and yet animate pluralistic social systems. The economy, especially the global economy, is a contact between culture and society: the economy is one of the social spheres and yet it also generates and mediates cultural meanings in the global field. This is especially true of transnational corporations.

A "transnational" corporation is an "agent" of global reach that faces the problems of production and distribution of goods and services. By its very designation, it is a community that transcends national political, legal, and economic boundaries. This means that a "transnational" is an economic entity that has freed itself from precommercial embeddedness in a specific nation's economy and culture. Whether or not modern market economies as such are "disembedded" from pre-commercial realities, this is clearly the case with transnational corporations. While it may be true that, say, IBM or Nike retain the cast of their "mother" country in terms of management style, tax law, and so on, these entities are free to incarnate themselves in different and quite diverse cultural contexts. The differentiation of social subsystems coupled with the disembeddedness of the corporation are preconditions for transnational corporate agents. This fact poses grave questions of economic justice. Given the capacity of transnationals to move under the pressure of the market — and thus endanger jobs, provoke immigration, create new possibilities of wealth — how does one speak about distributive and commutative justice?

The liberation of transnational corporate agents from precommercial embeddedness rests on widely held beliefs about human existence. Western cultures picture human beings as *historical agents*. This idea of persons is crucial for the shift to market societies away from tradition-based or authority-planned economic systems. Capitalist economies require the creativity of persons to produce and distribute wealth. However, there is a paradox facing market societies absolutely central to the remainder of my argument. The paradox, as many have seen, is that modern capitalism cannot insure its own presupposition. The more individuals are rationalized within the economy, the greater the social system undercuts its human condition. This is so, since market capitalism (1) presupposes that persons can (freely) dispose of themselves, and yet (2) commodification in the market and the reduction of all value to a monetary scale poses the question of how much I can sell of my labor, time, and body before I have sold off myself. The market tempts persons to dispose of themselves as persons. The market always threatens to devolve into "commercialism" where there is no "outside" to commodification. It becomes imperative, then, that one consider basic assumptions about human beings as historical agents and the extent to which economic institutions foster or destroy that agency. The great weight of the Christian tradition is to insist on the moral priority of persons over institutions and their practices. It is persons, not systems, that define the substance of justice.

Finally, the globalization of economic agents (i.e., corporations) has accentuated a fact present within all cultures. Any culture reproduces itself by informing the lives of its members in terms of some set of beliefs and values about the world and human life. This fact is most decisive. With the dramatic advance of the global media system and also the spread of transnational corporations, "economic values," along with money as the measurement of use, exchange, and sign value, increasingly permeate and define persons' and societies' self-understanding. Granted, corporations facilitate and enact goods other than purely instrumental, economic ones. The corporation fosters personal growth, the development of numerous virtues, a belief in fairness. And yet, because the corporation is defined by its specific economic purpose (wealth) and practice (production/exchange), it is always at the risk of reducing or effacing the difference between these various humane goods and purely economic ones. This is, again, the specter of commercialism but now at the level of value.

31

Transnational corporations are cultural forces — and not only social institutions — insofar as they foster and transmit a "table of values" that forms the self-understanding and agency of persons. Not surprisingly, within market societies it is increasingly difficult to give compelling reasons why something (say, persons or the common, social good) ought to be respected and enhanced other than in terms of their use-value in maximizing economic utility. Insofar as "money" is one of the languages or currencies of cultural reproduction in a market society, then there is always the possibility that everything can be made and measured as a commodity. Further, transnational corporations have become vehicles of the "moral imagination": they produce and distribute a table of values (beliefs about what matters in human life) that shape understandings and perceptions of life. By means of this connection to the imaginary, transnationals transform values such that systemic goods (e.g., wealth production) can endanger the worth of persons by commodification. The pressing question about the transnational corporation is not an economic one, but a matter of human purposes and value.

I have made three points about transnational corporate agents and have isolated questions of economic justice along the way. These points correlate to the meanings of "world" in Christian thought. First, we have noted the "locality" of transnational corporations, which transcend local political and pre-commercial relations. While this point can be made in terms of social theory — disembeddedness and social differentiation — corporations also demarcate a cultural space. It is a "space" of human life defined by market processes and values on a global scale. These entities are, quite literally, located in the whole world, the "ecumene." This is a simple descriptive claim about our situation even as it poses, in a new way, matters of distributive and commutative justice. Second, there is an anthropological observation. Corporations presuppose human beings as historical agents, and, further, they foster and yet also endanger that agency. At root this is a question of productive justice, both in terms of the presupposition of economic activity (i.e., human labor) and also how the creation of wealth coheres with basic beliefs about the meaning of our humanity. Finally, we have isolated an axiological point — a point about value — correlated to Christian convictions about creation and goodness: corporations, like all cultures, create and transmit some table of values. Those values always include a distinction between what has intrinsic worth and what has only instrumental value as well as the risk that this difference will be effaced.

The demand of moral responsibility in this situation is to communicate in and through the spheres of society the connection between selves and their own most intrinsic good. It is to provide a table of values about what lies outside of commodification. This is why the "world of mammon" is so morally ambiguous. It must be affirmed and curtailed at the same time. The problem of "the world" is that it is a domain of meaning and value that can contradict and war against the very source of its own meaning and value, namely God and persons. The conundrum of transnational corporations in a market economy is that they too can contradict the very source of their worth, that is, the dignity of persons. In grasping this point, we can return to the theme of justice and advance one more step to our conclusions about the church.

Responsibility in a World of Mammon

Our path of inquiry has led to the insight that the question of justice and transnational corporations must shift focus. Justice is no longer only a matter of the production and distribution of wealth or the morality of exchange, topics rightly explored by ethicists. *The question becomes the very place of a substantive sense of justice in our conception of reality and ourselves.* This sense of justice expresses the contrast between intrinsic and instrumental goods and is essential for resisting the utter commodification of life. Put in terms of economic forces, we must ask: Does the emergence and spread of transnational corporations — whether in terms of industry, electronic media, or other forms — provide any means for sensing the claims of justice as basic in self-understanding and a construal of the world? A Christian interpretation of the world is one mediated through beliefs about and experiences of the living God, the God of Jesus Christ and the prophets. Any cultural force or social institution that nullifies our sense of the reality of justice and mercy is, practically speaking, atheistic and, theoretically stated, nihilistic. If that is true of our economic situation, then Christians must advocate ways of containing and constraining transnational corporations. Conversely, if these economic powers do foster, or at least do not utterly destroy, a moral construal of the world, then Christian communities can find common cause with them and work for their transformation.

Admittedly, specific judgments about economic forces are often prudential and strategic in nature. There are times when economic agents will be demeaned in ways utterly destructive to any sense of justice and thus the demands of responsibility. In those cases, the churches must oppose economic powers. At other times and places, corporations might be agents of moral sensibility. This would warrant a (qualified) endorsement of their moral agenda. Granting the need for discernment in moral matters, the task of Christians, most basically, is to work for the transformation of the world around them. This moral stance admits the genuine ambiguity in all things human and yet seeks to work for their betterment. It is consistent with the account of the "world" found in Christian faith.

The transnational corporation as a vehicle of the moral imagination can aid in the formation of new social worlds as well as new forms of identity. This provides some means to ensure the dignity of persons even within economic practices. But that possibility assumes, of course, that our economic practices have robust images of human worth that can circulate within market societies. And this is where commercial cultures are failing most profoundly. The continuation and integrity of the economic sphere requires a table of values and a picture of human dignity in contrast to the ones found in these societies. Only through a different axiology operative at the level of how persons see themselves and their world may the tyranny of economic commodification be checked.

The difficulty is that it seems impossible to reach any consensus within pluralistic societies about the human good. The reason for this is not hard to grasp. In highly differentiated societies it seems impossible to conceive of an encompassing good that does not always tread on social tyranny, or, conversely, to provide reasons that are not sphere specific, that is, not trapped by the logic of any one social sphere (say, law, economics, or whatever). What is lacking is a discourse (a set of concepts, symbols, narratives) able to articulate intrinsic worth in a non-tyrannous and also non-sphere specific way. However, all is not lost. We must note something important. In pluralistic societies, each social subsystem is involved in distributing the primary good of membership in a human community. And this is so because membership is the presupposition of all other social purposes. Economic justice is, of course, about fairness of exchange, distribution of goods and services, and the creation of wealth within the economic sphere. Yet justice substantively defined is not sphere specific: *it is the demand, within each of the social spheres with their unique goods and practices, that the integrity of persons be respected and enhanced.* In order to practice justice so understood requires some way to imagine and conceive of the worth of persons *outside* or *prior to* their utility in social practices. Mindful of the role of the "imaginary" in the flows of globalization, the problem, therefore, is how to fashion self-understanding such that beliefs about the worth of persons, and thus the claims of justice, are properly basic. We need symbolic resources that can test and transform commodification.

Sensing the force of this demand, I have intimated a candidate for such an axiology, namely, Christian faith and its claims about "world," agents, and justice. The central Christian conviction is that all reality exists in relation to God as creator, redeemer, and sustainer, and in light of this fact, bears within itself an inviolable worth. This is most pointedly stated in the confession that God became incarnate in an embodied individual, and additionally, that Christ's spirit is communicated ecumenically in and through the life of the Christian community and its practices. The living God is never translatable into our system of signs, and morally speaking, this means that human worth, grounded in a relation to God, cannot be commodified or measured within the discourse of any social sphere. The church must transmit this picture of human life and enable it to penetrate the global social imagination. Christian faith provides symbolic and conceptual means to think about the very presuppositions of economic justice in ways that can form human self-understanding around the integrity of life. It provides a bulwark against the tyranny of any social sphere and its practices — a wall rooted in the worth of persons, consistent with a specific construal of the world.

In an age in which corporations have become global agents of the imagination, the most pressing question is really how we are to see and value the world. If we cannot see or sense the claims to respect and enhancement uttered in the lives of others, all the moral argument in the world simply will not help. So in the end, the task of the churches amid a world of transnational corporations is to provide an "outside" perspective on commodification and to form the moral imagination. To use biblical, prophetic terminology, it is a matter of "knowing justice." St. Paul put it even better: what is required is a renewal of mind so that we might prove the will of God (Rom 12:1-2). We must enter the school of Christ, the academy of justice, to have our lives renewed.

Christians must work to transform the patterns of value and means for self-understanding within commercial societies. How is that possible and how does it relate to the more proximate and pressing issues of forms of justice? The work of moral transformation is possible, I judge, because Christian faith and transnational economic agents share a presupposition, namely, that human beings are *historical agents*. The notion that human beings are owed moral consideration — counted as full members of the moral community — is not in principle contestable, even if it is always deniable. But from this simple fact about the subject of justice flow some important insights. First, the affirmation of human beings as agents warrants the importance of labor in life and thus the backbone of productive justice. To demean or destroy the conditions for human beings to labor meaningfully is morally illicit. To seek ways to enable persons to find fulfilling labor, and thus also the creation of wealth, is required. Second, the dignity of being a historical agent requires the empowerment of the poor to be a force in their world. That is, questions about distributive and contributive justice not only concern goods and services, they are more basically about how to respect and enhance persons as agents. For Christians and many others, goods and services draw their worth from their connection to human agents and not the inverse. And, finally, commutative justice is about how to respect and enhance agents within market exchanges. The morality of exchange is really about the interaction between persons who can knowingly shape their world and the kind of world they enact through the exchange.

These kinds of economic justice (productive, distributive, commutative) are various ways to respect and enhance the prior substantive good of economic systems, namely, human beings as historical agents. This moral good is necessarily binding on economic agents (like transnational corporations) because it concerns a presupposition of their very existence, a presupposition that is, paradoxically, also endangered by economic practices. The various kinds of justice may be seen as ways to allow Christians to live in but not become of the "world": *productive justice* articulates in economic life the meaning of creation as good; *distributive and commutative justice* enable the world of actual social and cultural existence; *contributive justice* reflects in economic life convictions about sin and redemption. All of these kinds of justice draw their moral force from a relation to agents, to the divine and human beings. The demands of justice for Christian faith focus on the presupposition of worldly value. Economic justice in its various forms is about respecting and enhancing the integrity of agents amid the world of mammon.

The Mission of the Church

These claims about Christian faith allow us to conclude with a word about the churches as ecumenical, worldly forces. If my argument about justice and the imagination is compelling, then the root mission of the churches is to work to inform the moral sensibilities of market societies so that claims to respect and enhance the integrity of life are basic to the self-understanding and ethos of a society. One ought not to be naive about this task. It is, quite simply, unending. And yet, it is the task through which the churches make their own moral history. It means that the best image of Christian mission in our time is neither missionary, nor resident alien, nor prophet voice. Of course, there are situations in which Christians must adopt these roles, and others as well. But on the example of disciples gathered around Jesus, the main task of the churches in a global future is pedagogical. It is to witness to the reign of God by teaching, learning, and living justice.

The ethical mission of the church is to be an academy of justice in the very crucible of culture creation. This vision of the Christian community is rooted in the confidence that, as creatures of a loving God, human beings can be grasped by truths that raise them above vice and hatred. In the end, the most powerful counterbalance to the "crisis of meaning" besetting postmodern societies and global reality is a simple and yet profound vision of individuals as agents of justice.

For Further Reading
Küng, Hans. *A Global Ethic for Global Politics and Economics*. New York: Oxford University Press, 1998.

Moltmann, Jürgen. *God for a Secular Society: The Public Relevance of Theology.* Minneapolis: Fortress Press, 1999.

Schweiker, William. *Power, Value and Conviction: Theological Ethics in the Postmodern Age.* Cleveland: The Pilgrim Press, 1998.

Walzer, Michael. *Spheres of Justice: A Defense of Pluralism and Equality.* New York: Basic Books, 1983.

2

The Debt Crisis in Theological Perspective

THE RIGHT REVEREND JAMES H. OTTLEY

Introduction and Theological Reflection

Globalization, and the economic and political forces associated with it, have dramatically changed the world we live in. Despite progress in technological advancement and signs of economic growth in certain places, poverty and underdevelopment continue to limit the bounds of human potential. The question of poverty has been discussed at many times in many places; however, people still seem to be unaware of the breadth and magnitude of this problem. In this regard, it is important to note the following facts:

- Presently 1.5 billion people live in absolute poverty. Most of these people go hungry every day. Seventy percent of these are women and children.
- More than half the people on this planet — over 3 billion people — earn less than $2.00 a day.
- 1.75 billion lack safe drinking water.
- 100 million are homeless.
- 800 million go hungry every day.
- 150 million are undernourished.

These alarming statistics reveal how much further we need to go to make this world a truly better place for all people.

In the fourth chapter of the Gospel according to St. Luke (4:18), Jesus puts the "good news to the poor" at the top of his introductory message. When the question was put to him, as to whether he was "the one who is to come, or do we wait for another?" Jesus responded, "Tell John what you have seen and heard . . . how the blind recover their sight, the lame walk, the lepers are made clean, the deaf hear, the dead are raised to life, the poor are hearing the good news . . ." (Lk 7:22-23). It is significant that in these instances, as in others, Christ's response is one of compassion to the spiritual, physical, and economic needs of those around him. When his disciples despaired because the multitude that followed Jesus were without food, Jesus' response was not to panic, but rather "make the people sit down" (Mt 15:35). Their needs were attended to in such a fashion that there were leftovers, even for others. God created the world and the world is good, which means that all of the creation is good and all of creation including its people must equally benefit from God's generosity. As God's people, we are called to use our minds and our hands to make this world a place that lifts up the dignity and values of all people.

U.N. Secretary General Kofi Annan, at the World Bank Conference in Toronto (June 22, 1998), said, "We are all here because we believe poverty to be intolerable in a world of plenty. And we are all here because we are convinced — indeed we know — that this poverty can be ended in our lifetime, with our own hands, with our own minds." He has also said, "So long as every fifth inhabitant of our planet lives in absolute poverty, there can be no real stability in the world" (Video message on the International Day for the Eradication of Poverty — October 17, 1998).

The Human Dimensions of the Debt Crisis

According to Gustavo Gutiérrez, the question for us is, "How do you say to the poor, that God's loves you/them? This continues to be a valid question when we observe the widened gap between the rich and the poor of the world."

I recently heard the story of a 50-year-old grandmother who lives in a two-and-a-half-room basement apartment with her pregnant daughter and three young grandchildren. Determined to provide a stable home for her grandchildren, this woman manages to feed, clothe, teach, discipline, and love them in spite of enormous odds. She does this even though drug trafficking and related violence are rampant in her neighborhood.

The reasons for her problems are many. Among them are lack of education, employment opportunities, health care, and community support. But the boomerang effect of the Third World debt crisis has aggravated her situation. The negative effects of reduced social spending and limited job creation have perpetuated conditions of poverty for many people. Many countries whose purchasing power was directed toward acquiring goods made in the United States and other parts of the world are now directing their spending toward debt service. As members of a global community which is increasingly interdependent, the crisis that disrupts the economies of trading partners eventually affects the economy here and elsewhere. Asia, Mexico, and the Pacific are recent examples. The point I am trying to make is that the problem of the International Debt Crisis has today become a global problem.

As these countries spend more money on the debt service, less money is spent on social and human service programs, which contribute to the total development of the whole person.

How do you say to the poor, under these conditions, that God loves them/me? The poor and working people throughout the world have suffered the most. A child born in Tanzania today inherits $250 of foreign debt. The Tanzanian debt is not renounceable; thus all citizens, even those not yet born, inherit a tremendous debt. Most of these people have had little to do with incurring the debt burden imposed upon them.

Most African countries have repaid their loans or debts. However, they are still paying in compounded interest from the past. Over 120 million people worldwide are officially unemployed; many more are underemployed. It should be noted that more women than men live in absolute poverty, and millions are refugees or internally displaced persons. This creates stability problems for both their home country and their host country. We thus need to recognize that on a global scale, political and economic violence has a spiral effect, exacerbated by the debt crisis.

For the sake of the children, and all of humankind, it is critically imperative that we seek ways to end poverty and hunger — that we fight unemployment, underemployment, war, conflict and violence, racism, sexism and discrimination; repression, oppression, human rights violations, and environmental degradation. At the center of all these ills, I believe, is the International Debt.

I recently attended a meeting sponsored by the World Bank, in which Alfredo Sfeir-Younis, the Bank's representative at the U.N., stated that the current key issues for the Bank are:

1. The eradication of poverty.
2. Environmental sustainability.
3. Financial development.
4. The negative impact of globalization.
5. Values; stressing what we believe in — how, as a society, we should move forward.

"The present situation of poverty is intolerable," he said, "and must be changed."

The bishops of the Anglican Communion meeting in Lambeth on August 4, 1998, in reference to the international debt and economic justice said: "We believe that God created a good world for all persons. It is a world in which we are bound together in our common humanity, formed in God's image and in which each person has equal dignity and value. With immeasurable generosity, God has given bountiful resources for all to share. We are responsible to hold God's gift in trust for one another seeking the good for all" (Lambeth Section 1.15).

This is a very important statement, for it lifts up and praises the generosity of God, the gifts of God to the world. A world with people of diverse cultures, wherein all are embraced by God's love, is a world where God therefore calls us, our minds and our hands, to be used for the benefit of all so that everywhere the people of the world may enjoy the benefits of all of God's creation. If this is to be a better world, then we must respond to the needs of the poor. The eradication of poverty must be at the top of our list.

Origins of the Debt Crisis

At this point we should refresh our minds on the "how" of the international debt crisis. You may recall that in 1997-98 there was a crisis of credit over supply. Here is how some members of the subsection on the International Debt Crisis at the Lambeth Conference refer to that crisis in a letter written to James Wolfensohn, President of the World Bank.

> The crisis arose from the accumulation of large surpluses by the oil-producing countries which the banks to which they are entrusted could not handle within the then existing lending system. According to Tony Thirlwall, Professor of Economics at the University of Kent at Canterbury, the consequent plummeting of interest rates threatened to bring on a banking collapse which would, in his view, have been quite as severe as that of 1929. The crisis was overcome first by adopting a newly elaborated system for banks to syndicate in order to be able to make sovereign loans; and secondly by a campaign, encouraged by the Bank and the Fund [the IMF], to offload the surpluses in loans to countries seeking development funds, attracted by the very low interest rates then prevailing. The primary motive at the time was not to foster development but to get rid of the surpluses. Although many of the loans were carefully placed and wisely used this was by no means the rule; some lenders did little to ensure that the borrowers would, if conditions changed, be able to service their loans. There was no standard provision ensuring that projects receiving major loans would contain a revenue-earning component. *(The Lambeth Conference, Canterbury; Reply to James Wolfensohn — August 1, 1998)*

Professor Thirlwall points out that the whole world-financial system and its structures benefited from averting the consequences of "credit" over "supply." He considers that equal benefit should mean equal sharing of the cost; but in this example the major cost was borne, and is *being* borne, by the borrowers; admittedly where banks had to make substantial provision for bad debts many small investors, particularly in mutual funds in the U.S., took losses on their investment (as they did later in the small banks and savings crisis); but their losses, though painful, were hardly comparable to the total loss of subsistence suffered by millions in the borrowing countries who, in any case, had no part in the decision to take the loans.

This situation cannot be laid at the doors of any of the presidents of the Bank or of their colleagues. But here is an issue of justice in which the Bank and the Fund are involved, and it ought to be taken into account in dealing with the debt crisis. So far as can be discovered from available evidence this has not happened.

Also contributing to the crisis were loans made without proper supervision; corrupt borrowers used loans intended for humanitarian needs for their own personal and military purposes. As a result, prices fell and interest rates increased, despite the fact that projections favored the reverse.

Lambeth's Response to the Debt Crisis

The bishops at the Lambeth Conference took the international debt crisis very seriously, and thus passed a lengthy resolution touching on the issues of the eradication of poverty, recognizing the work already done by political leaders, finance ministers, church leaders, and people of creditor nations and NGOs. I consider the statement important enough to warrant a detailed summary.

First, the conference recognized the linkage between the doctrine of creation and issues of international debt. As a matter of economic justice, we cannot view one another apart from our innate dignity as children of God and part of the divine creation: "God has generously given to the nations immense resources which are to be held in trust and used for the well-being of all." The fundamental way in which human beings ought to be in relationship with one another is not by means of lending and borrowing, but of free mutual giving: "Borrowing has its place only in as much as it releases growth for human well-being." Thus the power concentrated in lending institutions is misused if it does not stem the potential for damage resulting from a reliance on loans as a way of dealing with problems of development.

In that light, Lambeth praised the work done by international financial institutions and the G8 in focusing more conscientiously on Third

World debt relief. However, the efforts made thus far have been inadequate: "These measures do not as yet provide sufficient release for the hundreds of millions of people whose governments are diverting scarce resources away from health, education, sanitation, and clean water." The conference therefore called upon these institutions to begin the process of debt cancellation for the poorest nations, to grant them a degree of autonomy and to restore the credibility of their governments: "Debt cancellation is also a necessary step if these governments are to be given the dignity, autonomy and independence essential to the growth and development of democracy."

Lambeth called upon the leaders of creditor nations to take the following five actions:

1. To negotiate in good faith with debtor nations on the issues of loans and debt relief, recognizing the equal dignity of the citizens of those debtor nations.
2. To hold creditor institutions accountable to the governments under which they operate, in order to ensure fair lending practices.
3. To institute mechanisms for controlling bad lending practices and corruption within financial institutions.
4. To introduce fair trade policies into their relationships with debtor nations, thus enabling the debtor nations to better participate in the global economy and pay their debts.
5. To ensure that the member nations of the Organization for Economic Cooperation and Development live up to their promise to set aside 0.7 percent of their GNP for international development purposes.

However, recognizing that the debt crisis was not solely the responsibility of creditor nations, Lambeth also called upon the leaders of debtor nations to make the following four commitments:

1. To accept procedures for debt relief which are fair and independent.
2. To ensure greater legislative scrutiny of loan procedures, which will allow for greater accountability and more protection of the poor.
3. To develop methods for disciplining corrupt government officials who divert loan funds.

4. To develop policies which will make sure that the loan funds actually benefit the poorest in society.

Finally, Lambeth recommended that the United Nations develop a mediation council which will work on projects as diverse as identifying and eliminating unfair debts, to holding accountable those who engage in corruption.

These recommendations provide an important starting point for genuine debt relief which will recognize the legitimate interests of both the debtor and creditor nations. It provides a platform on which the churches can stand and from which the church may work toward the real alleviation of the poverty and misery caused by the debt crisis. Lambeth has provided us with an important starting point, from which we may continue to develop strategies to overcome the crushing burden faced by many emerging nations.

Conclusion

The issue of the international debt crisis has brought us to a very crucial place in our lives, wherein we have been forced to examine our values, our leaders, and our leadership. It has caused us to realize that we are indeed our brother and our sister's keeper. Mutuality and interdependence are a must if we are to live in a world where all people are respected — where the dignity, worth, and value of all God's creation must be celebrated.

Peace will come when we do what is right and good; when we act justly and walk faithfully with our God (Mic 6:8). When nations put away their machines of war, when nations beat their swords and spears into rakes and shovels; when nations decide not to lift up their swords against nations, nor ever again train for war, peace will come (Is 2:4). Peace will come when we use our minds, hearts, and hands to eradicate poverty in this world, so that the gifts of God's creation may be enjoyed by all.

References
Proceedings of the Lambeth Conference, Resolution 1.15 (available on the Internet at http://www.lambethconference.org/1/sect1rpt.html).

For Further Reading

"Called to Full Humanity: Study Document" (available on the Internet at http://www.lambethconference.org/1/report5.html).

Gutiérrez, Gustavo. *We Drink from Our Own Wells: The Spiritual Journey of a People.* Maryknoll, NY: Orbis Books, 1988.

3

Discovering a Role in God's Provision: Sustainable Economic Development for the Church and Poor People

DAVID BEFUS

A new missionary venture is started with an "emphasis that every Christian is a missionary and should witness through his daily vocation" (Dankar, 1971, p. 73). Missionaries work in exchange for their travel to the field, and all field expenses are paid out of indigenous income (72). Economic activities are considered "a trust from God, an aid toward fulfilling the tasks of the church, and a source of employment and community life" for the church.

The outreach of the church has often been connected to economic development. A foundation for knowledge about this connection might include academic research and field experience. I have worked for twenty-five years to promote economic development in emerging nations, and the cases cited here have emerged from my own experiences. Readers who would like additional information about the specific places and people to consult are invited to contact me (Dr. David Befus, President, Latin American Mission, (305) 884-8400, e-mail: drfebefus@lam.org). For anyone interested in this topic, the best thing to do is to come and see firsthand the exciting and innovative ways that economic development is integrated with church outreach. Come and see for yourself.

Principles and Practice —
Cases to Help Understand the Fundamentals

"In the beginning God created," we read in the first book of the Bible, and are told that God worked, and rested from work. Humans, created in God's image, also worked, providing oversight for God's creation. Work is part of the rhythm of the universe, even before sin enters the world. Provision for material needs is directly related to work. Once sin enters the world, productive activity takes on another dimension, requiring toil and effort, but the basic pattern of provision in relation to labor continues to this day.

As churches consider ways to reach out in ministry, some have used the creation of work opportunities as a basis for creating relationships. The FIME development loan program in the Dominican Republic has supplied loan capital to dozens of community banks that were organized in churches, providing a means for the church to respond to the needs in the neighborhood for income generation. From a ministry vantage point, the church uses a development tool, the community bank, as a bridge or channel to the neighborhood. As one pastor put it: "Most of the people here would never have entered the church door, because they find our singing and talking strange. But they came to the church to participate in a program to generate family income, and gradually became part of our church as well. Even if they do not attend Sunday services here, we consider them part of the family, and pray for them and take an interest in their well-being."

This statement was made by the treasurer of Banco Arca de Noe, who is not only the minister of the church, but also on the board of the community bank. His church is located in Tres Brazos, an urban squatter town on the outskirts of Santo Domingo. The community bank currently has sixty-five members, and a revolving loan capital of $17,800. Members of the bank meet monthly to evaluate individual and collective progress of the bank, and meetings also include opportunity for biblical reflection and personal sharing. Many business problems are actually symptomatic of spiritual problems, and in this regard, the church context provides full services, with counselors and prayer as well as administrative and technical assistance. There are twenty-one community banks organized in churches by FIME; there are others outside the capital city in Barahona and Jimani, very poor areas of the country.

The church involvement benefits the lending organization and the church, as the groups organized by churches have very low arrears and good reporting mechanisms. From a service delivery perspective, the church members are actually performing, on a voluntary basis, many administrative functions that are critical in oversight of loan programs. This also means that programs like this can provide very small loans and still be financially sustainable. This is a win-win proposition: the church obtains a valuable tool to help people in the neighborhood generate income, and at the same time the lending organization accesses voluntary services that allow it to reach the poor with very low supervision costs. The net result is to respond to people's material needs through the promotion of productive activity; to allow men and women to work, as God intended.

The theological emphasis of this program is on God as *provider*. The provision of God generally does not come by magic or miracles, but rather through productive economic activity. Abraham often states that "God will provide," and this is seen in animal husbandry and farming. When called to Canaan, or even when in trouble with the Egyptians, "God will provide." The provision of God for his people in the Old Testament is generally through agricultural production that requires work. The specific principle is presented often in Proverbs: "He who works his land will have abundant food . . ." (12:11; 28:19). It is also presented by the writer of Ecclesiastes: "so I saw that there is nothing better for a man than to enjoy his work, because that is his lot . . ." (3:22).

The teaching of these principles in the mass or church service is often accompanied by the painful realization that, in practice, there are so many other factors that affect God's provision for us. Some factors, like the weather, can be addressed only by prayer. Others, such as access to land, capital, markets, or production technology, may require assistance. As they say in Honduras, "a Dios orando, con el maso dando," i.e., we pray, and at the same time we keep hammering away.

The Caritas program in Juticalpa, Honduras, is an example of how the church has addressed the whole gamut of economic challenges facing church members. The nine parishes within a hundred-kilometer radius of the city of Juticalpa, an agricultural hub, can access loan funds for small agricultural projects, women's or men's groups, young people, and families. Interest is charged on the loans to cover both the costs of operation and devaluation. Most of the loans are for agricultural production, and are focused on investments that provide a cash payment, rather than on consumption crops.

This program has impressive financial statistics, but even more important is that it is integrated with other programs for health, spiritual, and community development that addresses the holistic needs of poor people. It also includes technical training to improve seed varieties, implement organic and environmentally safe methods for control of insects and fertilizer, and storage/marketing techniques to improve profit margin.

A Latin American Mission job creation project provides another example for us to consider. Its theological basis is the statement of the Apostle Paul: "Make it your ambition to lead a quiet life, to mind your own business and work with your hands, just as we told you, so that your daily life may win the respect of outsiders and so you will not be dependent on anybody" (1 Thess 4:11-12). Work is not only critical for providing for one's needs, but also the key to helping others.

The response in the squatter town of Chapulines, Costa Rica, was a project to make bean bag furniture, based on sewing that could be done within the home. The majority of the heads of households in this village were women, sole supporters of their children, and whose major need was income to provide for their families. They were unemployed, and in many cases unable to leave their homes. To lend them money would not have helped, as they did not know what to do with it.

The economic development literature calls this a "sectorial approach," but the missionaries and university student volunteers knew nothing of this, and were only trying to find a way for the women to "work with their own hands and not be dependent on anybody." The prototype models were made, raw materials purchased, and market outlets defined. The project was very successful, and many women also began making other products that they sold on their own. Gradually the management of all the business activity was transferred to the women, without outside support. The addressing of the economic needs of the community changed the Bible study atmosphere and deepened the relationships with the church.

Turning to another example, it is interesting to note that the early church had problems with its social assistance program, which was perceived by some as welfare for freeloaders. There were arguments about distribution of assistance (Acts 6:1). Paul is clear in his second letter to the Thessalonians that welfare freeloaders are not welcome: "He who does not work should not eat" (2 Thess 3:10). He presented his own example as a model. He was a leather worker, and as we know from Acts 18, made durable portable housing, called tents, but unlike our concept of camping tents. He promoted a model of sustainable self-reliance, even though he acknowledges that he had a right to donated funds. It was common practice for rabbis or teachers to have a skill to generate income, so they would not be completely dependent on revenue from their students. The skill that Paul had in making leather tents enabled him to generate income to support himself when needed.

In the same way, Pastor Julio felt God's call to be an evangelist, but could not leave the church where he was ministering because he needed the monthly salary, and he knew that evangelists made very little, beyond room and board. He heard about a loan program run by a Christian organization, and applied for a loan to start a ceramics business. He had investigated the business, and believed that it would be a great "tent-making" opportunity, because he already had experience making plaster-of-paris Bible-verse plaques, which he sold to bookstores. Investing in a small kiln and working capital, he taught his daughters how to prepare the clay, fill the molds, and heat the kiln. Over a period of a few years, he was able not only to support his ministry, but expand his business with a bigger kiln and full-time involvement of his children.

A variation on this approach is being used by missionaries in countries where there are restrictions on the open presentation of the gospel, for example, in China and Mauritania. These programs generate revenue, but more importantly they allow for the Christian message to be credible in a context where direct evangelization is not permitted.

To turn now to yet another model, we should remember that Jesus worked for many years in his father's business. Joseph is not referred to in the gospels, and because Jesus was the oldest son, some scholars believe that he may have run the family business for many years. That he knew the world of business is quite apparent from his statements and parables; his statement about the "wise man building his house on the rock" was not for a Sunday school song. And the statement in Luke 11 about someone who "constructs a tower without first studying the cost" demonstrates more than a little experience as a building contractor. He also spoke of workers unhappy with their pay, of employees who know they are going to get fired and use their last days on the job to prepare, of the handling of loan funds, and many other lesson stories based on the world of business. His teaching points out the degree to which he was acquainted with many of the fundamental productive activities of his day.

Just so, God provides for people through productive economic activity. Since the beginning of time, people have had to work to support themselves. This has been the plan since the creation of the universe, was evident in the example of God-made-flesh, and is God's plan for us today. Solidarity with the carpenter who prayed "give us this day our daily bread" implies that we too are called to engage in the life of productive economic activity.

Challenges for the Church in Promoting Economic Development

There are many ways to envision the process by which communities and people can promote "sustainable" development. For example, the practice of washing hands, boiling water, and using a latrine may represent a sustainable pattern that offers great benefits to people. In the same way, there may be sustainable patterns of community organization, and sustainable improvements in agricultural practices that affect the environment.

What people and communities want, at some point, is to also confront the issue of economics. One thing the poor have in common is a lack of money, although this may not be the first issue to address in community development. Health, community organization, and education are some of the foundations for productive activity, for people suffering from stomach pain are able to work neither very hard, nor very well. But once the basic foundation of social services exists, most people want to do something productive to support their own needs. Often community projects require surveys and forums to identify what the

53

people need for themselves, and the issue of economics generally comes from the community leaders, not necessarily from social workers or church workers.

A great advantage of church-related economic programs is that financial services can be integrated with other development interventions, as one part of a total package to address the needs of a poor community. Other organizations that promote loan programs do not have ways to access community groups, to build on existing educational and health services, or to combine financial services with other community programs.

The interesting result is that, as community development progresses, people in poor communities ask for assistance to do exactly what the apostle Paul has instructed: they want to work with their own hands, and not be dependent on anyone. But often they do not know how to do this. It is not easy.

A traditional response to the community interest in economic programs has been to provide production inputs on a donation basis. In some contexts, the donation is considered much more acceptable than a loan, not only because it appears to be consistent with donated funding, but also because it is possible to donate to people in an equitable fashion. Since there are no requirements, everyone is eligible. For example, many health projects offer primary care volunteers "income generating resources" as an incentive, without regard to entrepreneurial interest or ability.

There is also a related approach of providing "loans" but not really requiring that they be paid back. Much funding for economic activity in church and relief organizations continues to be either donated, or channeled to soft "loans" that are not tracked in relation to payback. The beneficiaries of these programs see them as short-term windfalls, one way that people can receive direct cash disbursements. In some cases, business activities are funded by donating assets or productive inputs rather than cash, but these assets can then be sold or liquidated; in many cases the entire production is consumed, without regard to additional productive cycles. For example, with food production, there may be project controls over the initial investment in planting, but no controls over what is done with the actual harvest.

Studies done in many organizations, and in the public sector, have consistently identified three basic problems with the gift/donation approach to economic activity: first, the underlying businesses funded are generally not viable; second, the donation has the tendency to not be valued; and third, a lack of discipline creates great incentives for fraud and mismanagement.

Perhaps the most damaging of the three problems is the fact that enterprises funded with donations are generally not viable in the real-world marketplace. Expectations are created, and the poor are handed another failure. For example, dozens of women are taught to sew, and provided with cloth, machines, and thread. But concern for quality output, response to markets, and adequate pricing is not included in the training. Once the sewing course is over, pictures taken, and budget spent, nothing remains except the memory of another failure. The donor agency can easily absorb the loss, even if the machines disappear. But what about the people who thought this would help them support their families?

All of the cases presented in the first section involve a clear separation between church and economic program service delivery. Loan programs have been a source of fraud in communities, especially if there is little or no tracking of what happens to the loan receivables, paid or unpaid. For those who do not pay, they learn the lesson that loans do have to be paid and promises kept — these are hard lessons. Funds invested in the program cannot be stolen or disappear somehow, but must be managed in a professional way with integrity. To prove that this is so, economic programs generally are run separately from church programs.

Church managers may see loan funds, investment capital, or interest revenue as the eventual source of cash to sustain the church administrative structures. In the case of FIME in the Dominican Republic, they have received thank-you letters from churches that have seen their offerings go up in relation to the community bank progress. However, what is put into the offering is voluntary, and there is no financial connection between the community bank and the local church operating budget. An interesting irony is that FIME, with so many banks operating out of churches, has a restriction on providing loans of any sort to pastors, as they have had too many problems collecting these loans.

The management of economic programs through separate entities helps to protect the church as well. The delivery of economic services is held at hand's length, and decisions on whom to help and not to help do not fall to the clergy. The need to promote collection of loans does not mix with spiritual and religious counsel, nor confuse motivations of laity, when performed by a separate entity.

Managing loan or business creation programs requires oversight and controls, and clear ownership definitions. A separate, specialist, sustainable entity is required to institutionalize financial services for the poor, and guarantee a disciplined system for recycling benefits to these people, after the initial intervention is over. This entity may or may not be registered as a legal parallel organization, but must be allowed to have its own management system and focus on its specific mission.

The church and its programs can function as a precursor for economic development programs. For example, training activities might take into account the need to prepare people for productive activity in the real-world economic environment. If the church funds small experimental projects for training, specific boundaries should be drawn in relation to beneficiary expectations, and the concept of graduating to a sustainable level of production should be encouraged. Technical training that promotes innovation and product quality should be encouraged, and the loan programs should support graduates of this training.

There are three specific levels for promoting sustainable economic development, beyond the subsidy or hidden handout stage. The first stage is to guarantee that funded proposals are viable projects in the real-world marketplace. The second is to demonstrate defined procedures, client lists, receivables tracking, and reports indicating that a formal service delivery program exists. The third stage is the presentation of financial reports that show how costs are covered by revenues in a financially sustainable pattern. A parallel entity, a legally registered organization with separate management, has proven the best mechanism for attaining these goals and serving the target population on a sustainable basis.

Separate, Specialist, Sustainable Micro Credit Entities — "Micro-Enterprise Development" (MED)

Governments of most countries support micro credit as a development strategy, and it is one policy that generally has support from politicians on opposite sides of the ideological spectrum. In the U.S. it is called "the only policy that appeals to the two Jesses — Helms and Jackson." A summit on micro credit was held in 1997 in Washington, D.C., that attracted participation from almost every country of the world.

The Grameen Bank and other large MED programs have eloquently presented the argument in favor of micro credit as a development tool. The poor want a "hand up, not a hand out." The poor are capable of managing loan funds on a very small scale, and paying them back. The cost per job created in the "informal sector" is far lower than the formal sector, and micro credit can address the pressing needs of those in the lowest economic levels.

Church-related programs may offer additional benefits. They may include integration with holistic community development programs, and be targeted at populations that are generally poorer than those of other MED agencies. They may take risks that others do not take, for example, in the financing of rural agriculture. They promote direct and indirect Christian witness along with financial services, recognizing the importance of the invisible world alongside the visible. They access other services for training and supervision from other church or parachurch structures. They also may be organized at very low costs due to existing administrative infrastructures.

The impact of MED programs has been especially great for women, who in many cases are the sole providers for their families. Women comprised more than half of the funding of many loan programs, not because there is a specific program that discriminates in favor of women, but rather because they tend to be better clients than men, more responsible in paying back their loans.

Some Christian development programs have rejected the concept of MED because they do not believe there is sufficient community participation in this program. Though communities generally participate in client selection and even board membership, this is considered insufficient. In some cases, the restriction of loans to only those that have viable projects is considered to be unfair. Sometimes national offices are unable to provide management support for the concept. At times the idea that the "community should make its own decisions" has been carried to the point where the national office cannot exert a leadership role. The separate, specialist concept of MED financial services is not appealing to some managers or national directors, as it takes resources out of their ultimate control: funds deposited for loan capital cannot later be accessed for operating expenses or invested in other types of programs.

A common barrier to success with micro credit start-ups is the acceptance of a discipline in relating costs to revenue. The tendency is to fill in the expense budget without filling in the loan disbursement requirements. This cannot be allowed, or expenditure patterns will eliminate any possibility of the program eventually becoming sustainable. This issue illustrates the fact that loan programs must be managed with a business mentality, and may require a different administrative culture than church organizations. Sustainable revolving loan programs are actually small banks, and must be managed as banks.

There are also ideological barriers to economic activity related to the church. The Bible is clear about the dangers of the love of money, but money itself is sometimes seen as the culprit. Business operates with money, and can therefore be seen as subject to all kinds of evil. Add to this negative image of economics the worries about capitalism, exploitation, risk, and possibilities for stealing, and many church managers would rather not get involved in economic programs. This is another argument for separation of economic programs in entities outside of the church, with distinct management. It also may explain why so little is written about integration of economics with church activities: perhaps it would not be well viewed by supporters and donors.

Doing Good and Doing It Well

Helping people to succeed in "working with their own hands" is a ministry. It is part of the testimony of Christians, for whom doing good is a sign, or as stated in one of the early letters, a fragrance. The letter Paul sent to Titus mentions "doing good" eight times, as the sign of the Christian. Micro credit programs are a great opportunity to do good.

Doing good also means doing a good job. The idea is that "whatever you do, in word or deed, do it all in the name of the Lord Jesus" (Col 3:17). The goal is to do the best we can. Church organizations need to approach economic goals for their members and other people with a concrete definition of micro-enterprise development, adequate performance standards, competent management, responsible means of governance, and evaluation and reporting systems. They need to do this because they want to do the best job they can. The advantage of a separate, sustainable, specialist approach to the promotion of economic development is that it continues even when church programs and emphasis change. The economic programs can attain sustainable levels, and be one truly visible sign of past involvement in helping the poor.

Long-range success also implies short-range complications. One of the most critical problems in the implementation of disciplined micro credit programs is that they require a complex management system. It is much easier to simply give things away; all managers ask for is a receipt to show that goods were purchased. When you lend funds, you need to know how they will be used. You need to train people to use them in a productive manner, so that revenue from the business, and not further indebtedness, is the source of the payback. The funds must be collected, and then channeled to someone else. These technical activities are what make the program work. This is what makes development work so challenging. For those who work in MED, they have all the complexities of big business, and none of its resources. That is why this kind of work is so much fun.

There are wonderful new opportunities for the small producer to participate in international trade, and *access markets* that were never anticipated. The knitted miniature soccer ball made in the Guatemala highlands can become a hit product in the U.S. and employ hundreds of women. Can the church play a role in helping the poor to find market outlets for their production?

The international standards for currency valuation have fallen, and the trend towards deregulation of economies seems to put all countries at the whims of the world financial system. This has brought a new type of *vulnerability* to international economic fluctuations, which is felt at all levels. What role does the church play?

It is said that the economy of the future is based on what you know, not on what you do, and the small producer also should be allowed in *new technologies* that are critical to maintaining competitiveness. But the rural areas of the developing world are very far from the urban areas, with no chance to connect to the electric grid, the telephone network, or the Internet. How can the church help?

The church has a special ability to promote economic activity that is also development oriented, by connecting economic programs to community development projects. But a strategic vision must now emerge for economic development as a worthy program in its own right, a ministry that is allowed to grow in meeting the needs of the poor to obtain their daily bread by working with their own hands. If we say that our mission is "to follow our Lord and Savior Jesus Christ in working with the poor . . ." we should seek to have the mind of Christ in discovering constructive roles to promote this. As it says in Hebrews 4:15, Jesus shared fully in our experience in living here on earth, including the workplace. His hands were just like the hands of the poor whom we serve. May these same work-roughened hands guide us, as we seek new ways to obey, and honor, and give him the glory.

For Further Reading

Dankar, William J. *Profit for the Lord.* Grand Rapids: Eerdmans, 1971.

Sider, Ronald. *Rich Christians in an Age of Hunger: A Biblical Study.* Downers Grove, IL: InterVarsity Press, 1979.

Stackhouse, Max L., et al. *On Moral Business: Classical and Contemporary Resources for Ethics in Economic Life.* Grand Rapids: Eerdmans, 1995.

Wogaman, J. Philip. *Economics and Ethics: A Christian Enquiry.* London: SCM Press, 1986.

II

FAITH, LEARNING,
AND FAMILY

Introduction

When we talk about globalization, we are talking, not only about a global economy or how this affects national economies or governments, but about all of the institutions that make up civil society — educational institutions, the family, the health care system, artistic institutions, philanthropic and charitable organizations, and many others. How the new global society that is emerging will affect these institutions is a subject of tremendous debate. On the one hand, old social formations seem to be breaking down or changing on a fundamental level, but at the same time, new formations are emerging which attempt to work constructively within the global society to preserve those institutions that are essential for human life.

Does the church have anything to say to the world in light of these changes? What is the church's own role as an institution of civil society in a global context? Christianity has a message, not only for the economy or for the state, but also for these other institutions. How can it make this message heard?

These concerns touch upon the subjects addressed in this section: education, the family, and worship. Each of these subjects reflects part of the matrix of Christian involvement in the public realm. Richard Osmer, in his essay "The Teaching Ministry in a Multicultural World," argues that, in a global society, the church must organize its educational ministry around its "perennial tasks" of catechesis, edification, and discernment. By focusing on these tasks, the church may move beyond merely parochial interests and respond with openness and integrity to the multicultural world in which it finds itself. Rather than diluting the gospel message, such a focus can allow the church to remain centered on the good news of Christ, and yet grant it the flexibility to respond to the movement of the Holy Spirit in an ever new and changing situation.

Mary Stewart Van Leeuwen's essay, "Worldwide Developments in Family and Gender Roles," looks at the effects of globalization on the structure of the family. Exploring this issue from within the Reformed theological tradition, she considers the evolution of the idea of the family as it has developed in the West in the twentieth century. Arguing that the prevailing models of family life have served to weaken it, she concludes that families are best served by those models which emphasize the partnership of men and women in a formal married relationship, but which do not attempt to relegate women to a separate subordinate domestic sphere.

The third chapter in this section contains worship resources, written by John Mbiti and edited by Tim Dearborn, that were used in the World Vision conference conducted at Princeton Seminary. The placement of these resources in this section reflects our belief that worship and prayer are the glue that holds civil society together. Part of our responsibility for the world involves not only analysis of institutions, or theological reflection, although these things are important. But a central part of Christian praxis is also the praise and worship of the Triune God of grace. John Mbiti offers us an example of how prayer and worship in light of globalization is possible. We invite you to make use of these resources in your own churches.

Both the essays and the worship resources in this section take very seriously the effect globalization has had on the institutions of civil society with which they are concerned. Yet questions linger. It remains for the church to explore in depth the impact of the global society on every facet of our common life. To what degree can local churches participate in and influence the changes that Osmer and Van Leeuwen point out? How can the church model the strategies proposed in this section? How can these recommendations extend to other institutions? These questions remain to be explored as we consider the role of civil society in a global era.

Scott Paeth

4

The Teaching Ministry
in a Multicultural World

RICHARD OSMER

Introduction

Preparing the members of Christian communities to participate in national and global communities that are increasingly multicultural represents one of the most important challenges facing the church's teaching ministry today. Contrary to those who argue that a relatively homogenous global culture is emerging under the influence of the media and market, I will argue that globalization results in enhanced multiculturalism, a sharpened awareness of indigenous cultural, moral, and religious identities. Does globalization necessarily lead to the homogenization of culture? On the surface, the answer seems obvious: "Yes!" The homogenization of culture is evident to the most casual tourist who has ventured outside his or her hemisphere and has witnessed the traffic congestion, high rise apartments, and fast-food chains around the world. Lying behind these surface manifestations are three broad-reaching trends: (1) the emergence of a global consumer culture in which standardized products are marketed throughout the world through an appeal to lifestyle preferences; (2) the spread of rationalized attitudes toward the world, largely fostered by the administrative needs of modern states and multinational economic organizations; and (3) the communication of idealized, Western

63

lifestyles through the global media, including television, movies, and music. Somewhat ironically, we will argue that the church can best respond to this challenge if it is clear about the core — what we will call the "perennial" — tasks of its teaching ministry.

Globalization: The Emerging Context of the Teaching Ministry

At first glance, these trends seem to indicate that the homogenization of culture inevitably accompanies globalization. In fact, however, the opposite may well prove to be the case. While the world has clearly become more closely linked through systems of transportation, communication, and economic exchange, fostering a common cultural veneer, it does not necessarily follow that this leads to a world that is more fully integrated. It can lead to a reaffirmation of ethnic, religious, national, and civilizational identities that take their shape explicitly in response to cultural homogenization. It is a mistake to view the Western image of globalization — the inexorable movement of humankind toward a secularized, capitalistic, rationalized, and democratic end-state — as the only form global reflexivity can take. It is far more likely that we will see the emergence of a wide range of cultural responses, a phenomenon that is already evident.

Especially important for our purposes is the role religion is playing in this process. Two closely related trends are apparent. The first is what Casanova aptly calls the "deprivatization" of religion: religion's refusal to accept confinement to the private sphere and its success in crossing over public/private boundaries to influence matters of political and social import (Casanova, 1994). A second trend is the rise of religious fundamentalism as a form of global reflexivity. In virtually all of the major religions of the world, this trend is evident. It is not uncommon for fundamentalism to cast its reassertion of tradition explicitly over against certain features of global culture: the materialism of consumer culture, the injustice of the international division of labor, or the hedonism of McWorld.

Is religious fundamentalism the only form religion can take under the impress of global reflexivity? This is an especially important question for countries that seek to maintain or establish democratic polities in the emerging global order. Religious intolerance, closely linked to ethnic or racial divisions, has become an exceptionally virulent force as globalization has accelerated. Is this the wave of the future? Does religion necessarily exacerbate racial and ethnic strife, making it difficult to maintain pluralistic, national societies and multicultural international communities? These questions bring us face-to-face with the tasks of the teaching ministry of Christian congregations. How might we conceptualize its perennial tasks in light of the challenges of globalization?

The Perennial Tasks of the Teaching Ministry

In an era of rapid and large-scale social change, the church would do well to remind itself of the perennial tasks of its teaching ministry. These are tasks that it must carry out in every age if its members are to make a faithful and effective witness in their own time and place. It is tempting to neglect these tasks in times of major transition, latching on to forms of education that seem more up-to-date or socially relevant. This may lead to a situation in which emergency "replanting" is in order.

The perennial tasks of the teaching ministry are three: (1) catechesis, (2) edification, and (3) discernment. While the church in all its ministries is changed with these three, the teaching ministry stands in a special relation to these tasks, ensuring that the members of the church acquire the requisite knowledge, dispositions, and skills associated with each. A brief overview of these perennial tasks will allow us to see how the emerging multicultural world poses a particularly demanding set of challenges to the church's teaching ministry.

By catechesis is meant the task of handing on the core beliefs and practices of the Christian tradition to every new generation of Christians and to Christian converts. While the term "catechesis" comes from the early church and not the New Testament, the task to which it points is given ample expression in Paul's use of the Greek term *didomi*, typically translated "to hand on." We find it in 1 Corinthians 15:3, where Paul writes, "I *handed on* to you as of first importance what I in turn had received: that Christ died for our sins in accordance with the scriptures, and that he was buried, and that he was raised on the third day in accordance with the scriptures. . . ." Paul uses this term several times in a similar fashion earlier in this letter (1 Cor 11:2, 23) and at other points in his correspondence to Christian communities. In 2 Thessalonians 2:15, for example, he writes: "So then brothers and sisters, stand firm and hold fast to the traditions that you were *taught* [*didomi*] by us, either by word of mouth or by letter."

Catechesis in the emerging multicultural world should be particularly sensitive to the content it hands on. Education is necessarily selective, and Christian education is no different. What contents of the Christian tradition are especially relevant to life in a multicultural, globalized world? Three doctrinal emphases come to mind: the Trinity, covenant, and reconciliation. Each is the object of renewed interest in contemporary theology in ways that make it an important resource for a church seeking to come to terms with globalization.

The doctrine of the Trinity, perhaps, has received the greatest attention in contemporary theology, leading one author to write of a "renaissance" of trinitarian theology (Cunningham, 1998, p. ix). The grammar of the doctrine of God is portrayed as balancing differentiation and unity, God's threeness and oneness. This has been developed in the direction of anthropology and ethics. Humans, created in God's image, are portrayed as inherently social beings. Moreover, the model of their sociality is in the perichoretic love of the Godhead, love in which the other does not negate the self but is necessary for its fulfillment. Otherness and difference need not be viewed as threatening but as a necessary dimension of the human condition. Belief in the Triune God, as such, opens out to human associations that find unity in and through differentiation, not in eradicating cultural differences.

Similar teaching potential is present in the doctrine of reconciliation. If this doctrine is viewed along the lines of an incarnational soteriology and does not focus exclusively on Jesus' death, then Jesus' many acts of reconciliation over the course of his earthly ministry can serve as potent resources for the teaching of reconciliation. What could be more important in a world that increasingly is torn apart by acts of violence and intolerance originating in cultural and racial differences? As Hannah Arendt once pointed out, it is forgiveness alone that has the capacity to break the cycles of mutual hatred that violence and intolerance breed (Arendt, 1958). Christians should be the first to practice forgiveness, not the last. This is not something that comes easily or naturally — hence, the need to give it explicit, sustained attention in the teaching ministry (see Jones, 1995).

The biblical theme of covenant, also, warrants special treatment in contemporary catechesis. In the Reformed tradition, this theme has been lifted up for doctrinal treatment in ways that have relevance to the challenges of multiculturalism in both national and global communities (see Stackhouse, 1997). Human associations of various types, both religious and secular, are viewed as covenants, relationships of entrusting and accepting entrustment involving consent and mutual obligation. Covenants, not contracts, are the standard by which social relationships should be construed. Stackhouse (1997), Allen (1984), and H. R. Niebuhr (1963) have developed this theme in the direction of a social ethic that can guide Christians in the family, the community, the marketplace, and politics. The standard in these arenas is not self-interest or self-fulfillment but an appropriate actualization of covenant love.

The second perennial task of the teaching ministry is edification. The New Testament term commonly translated edification is *oikodomeo*, which also is translated "to build up, improve, and encourage." Perhaps, the programmatic statement of this task is found in Ephesians 4:12, where Christ is described as giving gifts to the church "to equip the saints for the work of ministry, for *building up* [*oikodomeo*] the body of Christ."

A key to Paul's use of the term is found in 1 Corinthians 3 where he portrays the church as "God's building." He uses this image to describe the role of church leaders as being like specialized workers in the construction of a building. Each has something unique and important to contribute to the edification or up-building of the church, ruling out the sort of factionalism that had emerged in the Corinthian church. At a later point in this letter, especially chapters 12 and 14, Paul extends this understanding of edification to the entire Christian community. Here, he develops his well-known analogy of the body. In its diversity of spiritual gifts and ministries, the church is like a body in which every part plays an important role. All gifts and ministries are given for the "common good," for building up the body of Christ (12:7; 14:3, 12).

Edification is the task of building the body of Christ as a means of preparing the church for its mission in the world. One aspect of edification pertinent to globalization is moral education. More specifically, globalization necessitates the development of the cognitive dimensions of love: the capacity to construct and sympathetically enter the perspectives of other persons and groups and the willingness to view these others as having moral worth.

The importance of the cognitive dimensions of moral discourse has been articulated most forcefully in contemporary philosophical ethics by Jürgen Habermas (1990) and Seyla Benhabib (1992), and in practical theology by Don Browning (1991). As they point out, the pluralism of national societies and the multiculturalism of the global whole represent a major challenge to moral communities like the church, which make strong moral claims on the basis of their particular beliefs and ethical principles. How in the face of competing claims by other moral communities can they enter into a moral conversation in which the needs and interests of all are given their due? They point to two key conditions: the capacity to engage in general, reciprocal perspective-taking and the willingness to regard all conversation partners as having equal moral worth.

Moral conversation in pluralistic social contexts, however, requires two further steps toward post-conventional perspective-taking. The first step is the ability to reflect on the conventions into which one has been socialized, assessing them critically from the point of view of higher-order theories of knowledge. The second is the ability to temporarily set aside one's own point of view and enter sympathetically, but critically, into those of other persons and groups. Together, they allow reciprocity in perspective-taking: the ability to articulate one's own point of view as one among others and to enter into the perspectives of persons and groups who are different than oneself.

The second condition of moral conversation among pluralistic partners is the universalization of moral regard. It refers to an attitude in which all participants in the conversation are viewed as having moral worth. The achievement of general, reciprocal perspective-taking by itself does not constitute "the moral point of view." It can be used for purposes of manipulation and control in which the perspectives of others are taken into account solely for the achievement of strategic ends. How to ground this universalization of moral regard is a matter of considerable debate. Michael Walzer (1994) argues that justification of this moral orientation — no matter how abstract — inevitably rests on the beliefs and practices of particular communities. Indeed, every moral or religious community does not possess the resources to shape its members toward recognition of the moral worth of others. Even within a particular community, there may be arguments about how its traditions construe the moral status of those who are not its members.

I believe that Christian love, properly understood, opens out to the universalization of moral regard. Joseph Allen's treatment of covenant love represents an especially powerful argument along these lines (Allen, 1984, ch. 2). Christians are called to affirm the moral worth of the members of the various covenants in which they participate — not merely intra-communal covenants of home and hearth, but also, those forged in the marketplace, the political arena, civil society, and emerging forms of global community.

We now can give greater specificity to what is at stake in edification as moral education. Christian moral education, we contend, should support development toward general, reciprocal perspective-taking and the universalization of moral regard. In the limited time available, I will point to the implications of this position in two areas: parenting and congregational service projects. In contrast to those widely influential programs that encourage parents to break the will of the child early in life and maintain traditional patterns of female and child subordination to the authority of the father, the kind of parenting consistent with the position outlined above would encourage perspective-taking opportunities in the home and conceptualize all members of the family as having equal moral worth.

This is only likely to occur, however, if the congregation joins with the family in this sort of moral education. Congregational service projects oriented toward those outside the church represent and illustrate this point. Such projects can foster paternalism and even reinforce prejudice unless explicit attention is given to perspective-taking and moral regard in education accompanying these projects.

This sort of moral education in the home and congregation is especially important in a multicultural world. When it is present, edification is not an end in itself but a means of equipping the members of the Christian community to participate in God's mission to the world. The church teaches the kinds of perspective-taking abilities and universalization of moral regard that its members will need if they are to practice love in a world characterized by ongoing interaction with persons and groups whose beliefs and practices are very different than their own. In offering this sort of moral education, the church would make one of its most important contributions to public life, especially to democratic political and civil societies.

The third perennial task of the teaching ministry is discernment. Here too, we are pointing to something that stands at the heart of the Christian life and is not the concern of the teaching ministry alone. The teaching ministry, however, stands in a special relationship to discernment, helping the members of the Christian community acquire the knowledge, dispositions, and skills which it demands and providing settings in which it can be practiced. The New Testament term most frequently translated as discernment is *diakrino*, although *dokimazo* also is rendered discernment at times. It has a cluster of closely related meanings: to judge, separate, test, distinguish, and interpret. Paul uses the term in both narrow and broad senses. In 1 Corinthians 14:29, he uses *diakrino* to refer to the spiritual gift of interpreting tongues. More broadly, he uses it to describe a Christian leader's ability to judge disputes in the community (1 Cor 6:5). Its background is the legal sphere, pointing to the activity by which judges test and weigh evidence before rendering a verdict.

In both the New Testament and later Christian usage, the kernel of this legal background is retained. Discernment is the activity by which Christians attempt to determine the will of God in the face of a confusing or complex set of circumstances. It involves making judgments, examining the particularities of the situation at hand, and listening closely for the guidance of the Spirit in the context of Christian community. In both New Testament and contemporary understandings of discernment, however, the legal background is given a distinctive, eschatological twist. Christians are to judge the particular circumstances of their lives in light of God's future transformation of the world.

Discernment in this broad, eschatological sense stands at the heart of the Christian life. In all of its ministries, the church invites its members to engage in this activity. The teaching ministry, however, has the special task of preparing the members of the Christian community to engage in the discernment which other forms of ministry evoke. Across the ages, the church has taught practices — such as prayer and the spiritual reading of Scripture — that stand at the heart of discernment. It has offered moral education that teaches the ethical principles, patterns of reasoning, and dispositions with which Christians can think and act in situations of moral import. It has invited members of the Christian community to join with others in close-knit groups in which moral accountability, confession, and personal sharing play important roles. In these and many other ways, the church has made preparation for and the practice of discernment one of its perennial tasks.

Just as catechesis has as its goal teaching for faith and edification — teaching for love, education for discernment focuses on one of the central dimensions of the Christian life: hope. Discernment quickly becomes warped if it is not animated by a lively hope in God's coming transformation of the world, a hope that allows it to see hidden possibilities of transformation in the present that anticipate a fuller realization. Without this kind of hope, moral reasoning and acting quickly degenerate into legalism; prayer becomes little more than adjustment to life as it is; and the fellowship of small groups lapses into self-serving sharing. Hope is the animating force of discernment and the larger goal of this teaching task.

Prayer, as the seeking of God's will amid the complex circumstances of human life, lies at the heart of discernment. As a community of prayer, the church is reminded that its relationship with God is a living relationship and that God's commands come to it anew in the particularities of its own time and place. What often is missing from contemporary spirituality, however, is the eschatological orientation of Christian prayer. Jesus taught his disciples to pray: "Thy kingdom come, thy will be done on earth as it is in heaven." When this orientation is missing, spirituality runs the risk of cutting the Christian community off from the broader reach of its hope. As Jürgen Moltmann and others have argued, moreover, it has the potential of opening the church to a utopian impulse, the projection of imaginative alternatives that animate concrete engagement in the present (see Moltmann, 1967). That which the community of prayer seeks to discern is God's will for the present viewed through the lens of God's promised future.

There is, perhaps, no more important task before the church today than to live as a community of prayer animated by its hope in God's promised future. The forces of globalization are so complex and overwhelming that many are driven to attitudes of cynicism, despair, and apathy. The hyper-differentiated global economy leaves many feeling power-less to shape their own economic destinies. The sheer enormity of plane-tary issues like global warming and the spread of weapons of mass de-struction lead many to throw up their hands in resignation. A community of hope that prays for and works toward God's promised future represents an alternative. It discerns hidden possibilities of change in the present that can only be discerned by eyes of faith animated by hope.

How can the teaching ministry nurture discernment that is rooted in a utopian community of prayer? Three lines of education can briefly be noted. The first and most obvious is that the church should teach its members to pray. Public worship is especially important, for here the members of the community learn a grammar of prayer in the various parts of the liturgy (Saliers, 1984). The importance of public worship in teaching the community to pray places a special responsibility on the leaders of worship to consistently bring the concerns of the world before God on behalf of God's people. In so doing, they model an attitude of ex-pectation in which God's promised future guides the range of concerns that rightfully are brought before God in prayer. When this occurs, the task of the teaching ministry is to educate the members of the commu-nity in practices and disciplines by which they can reiterate in their per-sonal devotional life the same attitude of hopeful concern for the world they consistently find in public worship.

A second aspect of teaching for discernment is the use of the arts in education. This is one of the most underdeveloped aspects of the con-temporary teaching ministry, although signs of a new appreciation of the role of the arts have begun to appear under the influence of Howard Gardner's (1985) theory of multiple intelligences. Gardner argues that education too frequently has limited its attention to linguistic and logi-cal-mathematical forms of intelligence. Marshaling recent research on the brain and cognition, he argues that at least five additional intel-ligences can be identified: bodily-kinesthetic, musical, spatial, intra-personal, and interpersonal. Each has its own locus in the brain and its own developmental history. Education in the arts, he goes on to argue, plays an especially important role in nurturing forms of intelligence left untapped by the traditional three R's.

This brings us to a final aspect of teaching for discernment: explicit study of globalization oriented toward action that seeks to influence its course toward the purposes of God. Whether they work for a multinational corporation or simply watch CNN regularly, people are aware that changes of major proportions are taking place around the world. What they often lack is a higher-order perspective on these changes, something they are eager to gain. In teaching for discernment, the study of globalization is best linked to action-reflection models of education. These models invite persons to press beyond study alone to effect concrete responses to the issue on which they are focusing. Action informs reflection, and reflection guides action. Discernment becomes more than an idle intellectual exercise. It becomes a way of shaping one's life and world in response to new understanding of God's purposes.

Such action frequently is the seedbed of hope, for it breaks the cycle of passivity and resignation that large-scale institutional forces often engender. It commonly has the effect, moreover, of pressing persons back to prayer, as it becomes evident that working for change in the face of global forces can seem minuscule and be costly. It is here, perhaps, that prayer for the coming of God's promised future becomes most needed and most desired.

Conclusion

In this chapter, a comprehensive framework for the teaching ministry of congregations has been developed. Three perennial tasks of this ministry have been identified: catechesis, edification, and discernment. Each task has been conceptualized in relation to the emerging global context. This framework is best viewed as offering guidelines for congregations to assess their own educational programs, helping them determine areas of strength and weakness. As the church moves into the new millennium it would do well to reflect on the kind of teaching and learning its members will need if they are to make a faithful and effective witness in a world that is rapidly globalizing. For the church to change, it must remain the same.

Works Cited

Allen, Joseph. *Love and Conflict: A Covenantal Model of Christian Ethics.* Nashville: Abingdon, 1984.

Arendt, Hannah. *The Human Condition.* Chicago: University of Chicago Press, 1958.

Benhabib, Seyla. *Situating the Self: Gender, Community and Postmodernism in Contemporary Ethics.* New York: Routledge, 1992.

Browning, Don. *A Fundamental Practical Theology: Descriptive and Strategic Proposals.* Minneapolis: Fortress Press, 1991.

Casanova, Jose. *Public Religions in the Modern World.* Chicago: University of Chicago Press, 1994.

Cunningham, David. *These Three Are One: The Practice of Trinitarian Theology.* Malden, MA: Blackwell, 1998.

Gardner, Howard. *Frames of Mind: The Theory of Multiple Intelligences.* New York: Basic Books, 1985.

Habermas, Jürgen. *Moral Consciousness and Communicative Action.* Cambridge, MA: MIT Press, 1990.

Jones, Gregory. *Embodying Forgiveness: A Theological Analysis.* Grand Rapids: Eerdmans, 1995.

Moltmann, Jürgen. *Theology of Hope: On the Ground and the Implications of a Christian Eschatology.* New York: Harper & Row, 1967.

Niebuhr, H. Richard. *The Responsible Self.* New York: Harper & Row, 1963.

Saliers, Don. *Worship and Spirituality.* Philadelphia: Westminster Press, 1984.

Stackhouse, Max L. *Covenant and Commitments: Faith, Family, and Economic Life.* Louisville: Westminster/John Knox Press, 1997.

Walzer, Michael. *Thick and Thin.* Notre Dame: University of Notre Dame Press, 1994.

For Further Reading

Foster, Richard. *Prayer: Finding the Heart's True Home.* San Francisco: Harper & Row, 1992.

Gardner, Howard. *Art, Mind, and Brain.* New York: Basic Books, 1982.

Osmer, Richard. *A Teachable Spirit: Recovering the Teaching Office in the Church.* Louisville: Westminster/John Knox Press, 1990.

Thompson, Marjorie. *Soul Feast: An Invitation to the Christian Spiritual Life.* Louisville: Westminster/John Knox Press, 1995.

5

Worldwide Developments
in Family and Gender Roles

MARY STEWART VAN LEEUWEN

Introduction

The term "globalization" is used to mean many things, both in the church and in the world at large. Within the church, it can refer to worldwide ecumenical efforts to resolve matters of doctrine and service, to the global challenge of doing responsible evangelism, or to the growing global, interfaith dialogue among adherents of the world religions. More generally, globalization refers to the worldwide spread of modernity in the form of democracy, technological rationality, market-oriented economics, and urbanization, and to the resulting changes in institutions such as the media, government, law, medicine, education, and the family.

The focus of my presentation is the last of these — namely, the effect of modernity's global reach on gender and family relations, both in the more industrialized and the still industrializing parts of the world. I consider globalization, gender, and the family in terms of a Reformed world and life view, and also as mediated by the second wave of feminism, which I take to be one of many forms of "reflexive" globalization. By this I mean a social movement that responds critically to selected outcomes of political, economic, technological, and cultural globalization, with a view to altering those outcomes. Global feminism is thus parallel in form, though different in focus, to other forms of global activism, such as the peace movement, the environmental movement, and certain forms of religious fundamentalism, each of which criticizes certain aspects of modernity while at the same time availing itself of many other aspects in the process of disseminating its agenda and realizing its goals.

Preliminary Theological Comments

I begin with some remarks on the theological framework with which I approach my topic. From the perspective of a Calvinist Christian working in the tradition of Abraham Kuyper, two biblical-theological themes are particularly relevant. The first is the Reformed doctrine of the cultural mandate, and the second is Reformed theology's perennial reminder that human activities and institutions are at one and the same time blessed in creation and distorted by sin.

The *locus classicus* for the doctrine of the cultural mandate is Genesis 1:26-28:

> In the image of God he created them; male and female he created them. God blessed them and said to them: "Be fruitful and multiply, and fill the earth and subdue it; and have dominion over the fish of the sea and the birds of the air and over every living thing that moves upon the earth."

Note well: we do not find God saying to the first female "Be fruitful and multiply" and to the first male "Subdue the earth." Both mandates are given to both members of the primal pair. Both are called to accountable dominion, sociability, and responsible procreation. Made jointly in the image of God, both women and men are called to unfold the potential of creation in all areas of life. Together they are to work out God's call to stewardship, justice, and fidelity in ways that are sensitive to different settings and times in history, and to the life cycle of male and female human beings. None of this is necessarily incompatible with a gendered division of labor, which is something that we see to a greater or lesser degree in every human culture. But it does imply that wherever there is a construction of gender relations based on an exaggerated or inflexible separation of the cultural mandate by sex, we can expect trouble in the long if not the short run, because such an arrangement is creationally distorted and therefore potentially unjust towards both sexes. The cultural mandate is a human, not a gendered mandate.

Modernity gave us an example of just such an exaggerated separation of the sexes in the nineteenth-century "doctrine of separate spheres," whereby it was assumed, in the wake of industrialization and urbanization, that women should be "angels of the home" and men should be "captains of industry" — and of commerce, politics, and the academy. The resulting family form, which remained the societal ideal through the 1960s — and which the West also exported to the less-industrialized world in its development policies — was ironically known as the "traditional" family. Ironic because, in the long sweep of history the truly traditional family is one in which workplace, dwelling space, and child-rearing space largely coincide for both husbands and wives: think of your ancestors who ran family farms, or family businesses with living quarters above or behind the shop. Ironic too because even at the height of its acceptance, many people — especially rural, poor, and working-class people — could not afford to buy into the single male-breadwinner model represented by the doctrine of separate spheres. And whatever else divides feminists of differing ideological stripes and cultural backgrounds, most are united in the conviction that in the interests of gender justice the doctrine of separate spheres needs to be greatly modified, if not completely dismantled.

With regard to my second theological theme, the tension between created goodness and the distortion of sin, it bears repeating that marriage is part of God's created order. That it is meant to be a lifelong, one-flesh, monogamous union is affirmed in the creation accounts and reaffirmed in the Gospels (e.g., Mk 10, Mt 19, Lk 16) and the Epistles (e.g., 1 Cor 5 & 7, Eph 5, 1 Tim 3, Titus 1). The New Testament also makes it clear that persons do not have to marry in order to carry out the cultural mandate in cooperation with others, and Protestant Christians especially tend to forget this. Nevertheless, marriage is part and parcel of what God has approved for human life on earth, reflecting the cooperative, unity-in-diversity of Father, Son, and Holy Spirit, and the means by which future imagers of God are to be procreated.

However, like all creation structures peopled by fallen human beings, marriage and family are the potential locus of much sin. As Christians strive to reaffirm the normativity of the committed, heterosexual, two-parent family, they are often tempted to romanticize it as a "holy refuge" or a "haven in a heartless world." But the biblical record is full of accounts that tell us otherwise — records of family feuds and the sexual weaknesses of a host of Old and New Testament notables of both sexes. And today, as a member of my own denomination's recent Synodical Committee on Abuse, I can affirm that the prevalence of physical, psychological, and sexual abuse in churched families is pretty much the same as in the North American population at large.

So in terms of biblical theology, all families — including intact, two-parent Christian families — are most accurately likened to the little girl of nursery rhyme fame: when they're good, they're very, very good, and when they're bad, they're horrid. We have no theological brief to defend a romanticized view of marriage and families, in our own or any other culture. Marriage and family life, like all human relations, require hard work, self-insight, and a willingness to listen, forgive, and grow. At the institutional and public policy level, they also require a capacity to discern the shape of social justice, not measured against some rigid, atemporal set of gender and generational roles, but according to a biblical vision of shalom which will necessarily play out somewhat differently in different times and cultures.

Models of Marriage in the Twentieth Century

Although this vision of marriage and family rejects a rigid division of activities by gender, it retains the view of marriage as based on sexual complementarity, a view that was formalized in English common law and church cannon law as far back as the middle ages. In this view, marriage is an institution — a whole that is more than the sum of its parts, and a sexual community in which the nurture of children, by procreation or adoption, is a central function. It sees marriage as the basic social institution through which men and women unite lives, establish families, and form intergenerational bonds. In Reformed parlance, it is a "sovereign sphere" which has its own integral character and task, and is meant to work with (and not be overwhelmed by) other institutions — such as commerce, science, education, or government — to form a just and healthy society.

In the West and increasingly in the developing world, two other models of marriage now compete with the complementarity model. Until recently, the most viable competitor has been the liberal or choice model, according to which marriage is not a social institution, but simply a contract between individuals, the purpose of which is to maximize personal fulfillment, sexual and otherwise, and which can be broken whenever either party decides (for whatever reason) that its costs outweigh its benefits. It assumes a universe in which social order and obligation proceed not from created norms, but from personal choice in the private sphere and majority rule in the public. On this view, rights are attached to free-floating individuals detached from any social context. It is fair to say that, with the advent of no-fault divorce (which in effect allows unilateral divorce) the liberal model has largely replaced the complementarity model as the assumed legal and ethical framework for marriage in the West, despite a growing literature on the negative effects of divorce for both the children and adults involved.

However, a third, "postmodern" model of marriage and family is now emerging which tries to mediate between the first two. This model rejects the rugged individualism of the liberal model in recognizing that human beings are social creatures who need stable relationships. Its adherents view marriage as ideally a long-term interpersonal and sexual partnership — albeit a socially constructed one which takes different forms in different cultures — whose purpose is to encourage intimate and mutually nurturant relationships which link couples and households to wider communities. But it differs from the first model in its insistence that marriage need not be based on sexual complementarity, but simply on the right of all persons to participate fully in the institutions of society and their accompanying benefits.

Thus, in the postmodern model, it is only the motivation for being in a committed sexual relationship that matters. The sex of the persons is irrelevant. Hence the legal, cultural, and religious benefits of marriage should be available to anyone wishing to make such a commitment. Political activists and social scientists endorsing the legalization of gay marriage and parenting seem to assume a postmodern model of marriage, as do those in mainline churches who support religious ceremonies for same-sex unions.

In the developing world, the forces of modernity have changed gender and family relations in ways that mirror, with a predictable time lag, their effects in the West. Especially pertinent is the effect of exporting the doctrine of separate spheres to pre-industrial countries from the late nineteenth century on. Under pre-colonial systems of gender complementarity, women usually had independent access to economic resources (such as land) and were expected, like the women in premodern Europe and America, to provide certain goods and services to the immediate and extended family. But under the economic growth paradigm of development which held sway till about 1970, cash cropping and the giving of land titles and development aid primarily to men resulted in women losing access to these traditional resources. At the same time they were largely denied access to new resources (credit, fertilizer, etc.) that would ensure that their productivity continued to match that of men, in degree if not in exact kind.

Ironically, such policies tended to weaken rather than strengthen family life: less food was being produced all round, women had to ask their husbands for resources they once supplied alongside them, and males began to desert families they were unable to support economically by themselves. Thus, despite differences in details and timing, the forces of global modernity have thrown up similar challenges to gender and family relations in both the industrial and the developing nations. These include the breakdown of economic cooperation between the sexes and generations, and the increasing de-institutionalization of marriage as seen in growing rates of divorce, temporary cohabitation, out-of-wedlock childbearing, male migration and family desertion, and the acceptance of homosexuality as an alternative lifestyle.

Competing Models of Marriage and Gender Relations for the Twenty-First Century

There are four main responses to the state of gender and family relations as summarized above. From a feminist point of view, two of these are non-starters, and in terms of a Reformed worldview the other two — which we find combined in the theoretical and empirical work of the United Nations Development Program (UNDP) — need theological nuancing in order to be acceptable.

The first two options represent the forces of reaction, one of which explicitly aims to reinstate both a gender hierarchy and a highly gendered public/private dichotomy. It is most dramatically exemplified in the parts of Afghanistan presently under control of the Muslim Taliban forces, who forbid females from going to school, working in the public arena, or even going out in public unaccompanied by a male relative. The second, equally reactionary force is the so-called voice of cultural preservation, and it comes from a quite different quarter — namely, that of academic postmodernism, whose ranks include cultural relativists of a curiously absolutist sort. Under the rubric of opposition to Western imperialism and essentialism, these (mainly Western) scholars seem determined to romanticize cultural difference even when the results for girls and women include educational deprivation, unequal health care, and premature death due to dowry murders or female circumcision operations gone awry. Both of these positions of reaction are indifferent — in practice if not in principle — to any discussion of human justice that might transcend the distinctions of culture and gender.

A third "functional equality" model (presently most fully implemented in the Scandinavian countries) draws strongly on the traditions of liberal feminism. In opposing the doctrine of separate spheres, it negates the very idea of gender roles and calls for domestic activities to be evenly divided between spouses or contracted out to third parties. This model also favors waged labor for wives as well as husbands (with the state underwriting the resulting need for child care) and regards the individual rather than the married couple as the unit of assessment for both taxation and pension purposes. However, although this model represents an understandable reaction to a pre-feminist, gendered public/ domestic dichotomy, it ends up being just as restrictive as the latter in its attempt to make every couple and family operate in the same way.

The fourth, or "social partnership" model, aims for more flexibility than either of these two extremes. Like the historically long-standing complementarity model, it sees the family as more than the sum of its parts — as a corporate unit that confers ongoing rights and obligations on all its members. It calls for marital flexibility in the division of waged and unwaged work, but in either case allows for some kind of family allowance or tax subsidy to aid with the costs of child care, whether undertaken at home or contracted out. It also calls for credit-sharing of all pension assets, meaning that husband and wife have ongoing, joint title to accumulating public and/or private pension funds. This is particularly important in preventing the impoverishment of a homemaker spouse in the event of divorce. Finally, supporters of this model recognize that time taken out of the waged workforce for family reasons will reduce a person's earning capacity and accumulated pension, and thus they recommend "homemakers pension credits" for years spent in non-waged caregiving by either spouse. However, some advocates of the partnership model are agnostic on the need for formalized, heterosexual marriages, and see the partnership model, with its benefits and responsibilities, as equally applicable to any cohabiting couple, whether gay or straight.

The UNDP on Gender and Family Relations

The UNDP is a global development program whose model for gender and family relations draws strongly on the third and fourth models described above. It is based on a "human capabilities" approach that first, goes beyond mere monetary indices of national prosperity and second, embraces a model of human flourishing which leaves room for cultural differences without embracing total cultural and ethical relativism. Thus, since 1990 the UNDP's annual Human Development Index (HDI) has compared nations in terms of average life expectancy, educational attainment, and real personal income. Interestingly, nations with high Gross Domestic Products (GDPs) do not necessarily score high on the HDI, nor do nations with modest GDPs necessarily score low. Greater national wealth does not necessarily translate into shared "people benefits," nor does modest national wealth prevent motivated nations from sharing its benefits equitably.

More recently the UNDP has developed a second measure — the Gender-Related Development Index (GDI) which is basically a nation's HDI discounted for gender inequality — i.e., by comparing women's average life expectancy, education, and income to those of men. According to these measures, no nation treats its women as well as its men, although the Scandinavian nations come closest. And as with the HDI, Gross Domestic Product (GDP) is not necessarily a good predictor of a nation's record regarding gender equity. But the human capabilities approach required yet another step, because a high GDI may still not translate into women's empowerment in the public realm. Thus in 1995 the UNDP developed the GEM, or Gender Empowerment Measure, a composite index which ranks nations on women's per capita income, on the proportion of those holding managerial/professional or administrative/technical jobs who are women, and the proportion of those holding seats in the national parliament who are women.

By comparing countries' rankings on the GDI and GEM, one can see which nations have not just strengthened women's capabilities through access to health, education, and basic income, but which have opened up opportunities for women in the public spheres of business, industry, and national politics. Almost no country's GEM is as high as its GDI, showing that globally women's empowerment in the public sphere lags behind their access to basic human capabilities.

How are we to evaluate the UNDP's attempt to assess gender equity globally? The HDI, the GDI, and the GEM are obviously limited measures of human flourishing and gender equity: they do not, for example, include measures of family stability or of religious and political freedom. Yet the human capabilities approach has avoided the pitfalls of postmodern cultural relativism, while allowing for some variation in the way that distributive justice plays out cross-culturally. But in choosing to focus on women's progress in the public sphere, the GEM follows the functional equality model in assuming that gender equity always requires equal public participation by women and men. And like the functional equality model, the GDI and the GEM assume that individuals, not families, are the only relevant units of comparison.

However, some agencies (e.g., USAID) and even some feminist scholars have been more favorable to the idea of using intact families as the unit of analysis for development theory and practice, provided that intra-family dynamics concerning resources and bargaining power are considered alongside the goals of economic development and family preservation. Development is not a gender-neutral practice, and too often in developing countries men's control over family labor and earnings is used to enhance their individual welfare at the expense of other family members. Any development scheme is likely to founder if it ignores this asymmetry and does nothing to counter it by increasing women's resources, whether in terms of training, access to credit, or access to needed tools, land, and other materials. This does not necessarily need to translate into the encouragement of completely androgynous roles, as recommended by the functional equality model. But it does mean emphasizing reciprocal obligations and equitably shared benefits between spouses, and this cannot happen if women lose their access to traditional resources and at the same time are denied access to new ones.

In addition, the otherwise-laudable partnership model needs to take seriously the normativity of heterosexual marriage. Although no one denies that divorce and single motherhood are the lesser of two evils where there is a chronic pattern of abuse, addiction, adultery, or financial irresponsibility, there is nevertheless an accumulating body of empirical evidence showing the benefits of egalitarian, heterosexual co-parenting for women and children alike. Scott Coltrane's work on an ethnographic database of close to a hundred pre-industrial societies has shown that the cultures where fathers show the most affection, proximity, and responsibility for children are also the ones which are likely to support female participation in community decision making and female access to positions of authority. Men in such cultures are less apt to affirm masculinity through boastful demonstrations of strength, aggressiveness, and sexual potency, to entertain an ideology of female inferiority, or to practice dominating behavior towards women.

So from the perspective of a Reformed worldview, the most promising vision of gender and family relations is a combination of the partnership and complementarity models. In industrialized countries, a fully developed partnership model allows for flexibility in the ways families divide labor in both public and private spheres, while ensuring that the fruits of that joint labor are equitably shared by all. In less industrialized countries dependent on external development aid, the partnership model can work equally well provided that both visible and invisible economic contributions of all family members are taken account of, and the economic expectations of both men and women are backed by the development resources that allow both to have a true stake in the production and enjoyment of family wealth.

But inasmuch as the partnership model does not affirm heterosexual co-parenting, it needs to draw from the older complementarity model. Children of both sexes need stable, nurturant adult role-models of both sexes to better develop a secure gender identity which then allows them (as Scott Coltrane's work has shown, along with the work of feminist object-relations theorists) to relate to each other as human beings, rather than as reduced, gender-role caricatures. This does not require that such role-models always and only be the child's biological parents. But it strongly suggests that, whether in industrial or developing countries, there are limits to the diversity of family forms we should encourage around the core norm of egalitarian, role-flexible, heterosexual co-parenting.

For Further Reading

Cahill, Lisa Sowle. *Between the Sexes: Foundations for a Christian Ethics of Sexuality.* Philadelphia: Fortress Press, 1985.

Everett, William. *Blessed Be the Bond.* Philadelphia: Fortress Press, 1985.

Post, Stephen. *Spheres of Love: Toward a New Ethic of the Family.* Dallas: SMU Press, 1994.

Stackhouse, Max L. *Covenant and Commitments: Faith, Family and Economic Life.* Louisville, Westminster/John Knox Press, 1997.

Van Leeuwen, Mary Stewart. *After Eden: Facing the Challenge of Gender Reconciliation.* Grand Rapids: Eerdmans, 1993.

———. *Gender and Grace: Love Work and Parenting in a Changing World.* Downers Grove, IL: InterVarsity Press, 1990.

6

Resources for Worship

REV. PROF. JOHN MBITI

Introduction by Tim Dearborn

The primary response of the church in all situations is worship. In worship we affirm that there is but one Lord, one Truth, one Hope, and one Baptism. In worship we affirm that we are not gods, not masters of our own future, not sovereign in the affairs of history. In worship we thus affirm our confidence in the Lord of history, the Lord of the future, and celebrate the certainty that our globe is in God's hands. Further, in worship we affirm the conviction that what unites us is far more determinative of our lives than all that divides us. We are bound together as common creatures in the image of our Creator.

Rev. John Mbiti is a theologian, pastor, and missiologist who has led God's people in worship throughout the world. He has prepared the following three liturgies as resources for churches as we worship the God of the universe. They can be used in their entirety, or selections can be excerpted and included in worship services. May God richly bless our giving voice to Creation's praise.

*   *   *

Service of Worship

Call to worship (Liturgist)

"I was glad, when they said to me, 'Let us go to the house of the Lord!'
  Our feet have been standing within your gates, O Jerusalem . . ." (Ps
  122:1).

Let us stand up and continue our service:

LITURGIST: O, Lord, open my lips.
PEOPLE: And my mouth shall proclaim your praise.
LITURGIST: The Lord's unfailing love and mercy never cease.
PEOPLE: Fresh as the morning and sure as the sunrise.

LITURGIST: *Instruction:* During the next portion of our morning prayers
  I want each of us to choose one arm, whichever it is, left or right —
  which you then *strictly* refrain from using, until I tell you to use it
  again. Please be strict with yourself about this. Do it now.

Before we sing Psalm 100, I want each of us to turn to the next person
  and, keeping one arm away, embrace that person to greet him or
  her. Again,
  The greeting — embracing.
  Psalm 100: the cantor sings the verses and we all sing the refrain.

Scripture Reading Matthew 12:9-13
LITURGIST: The Word of the Lord.
CONGREGATION: Thanks be to God.

Meditation

Jesus enters the synagogue. In the congregation, there is a man with a
withered hand. Yes, also in this congregation there are twenty, forty, seventy men and women, with withered hands. How does it feel, to have
(symbolically) a withered hand or arm? Does that say something about
our life, our ministry, and our mission, when God's people have withered hands?

  What can become withered in our lives: the arm, the hand, the eye,
the ear, or the leg? What about withered love in our families? Nearly half

87

of the marriages in this country end in divorce. What happens to the other half of love between husband and wife? A high percentage of children (about one-third) are brought up by one parent. Where is the other half of parental love?

We can raise similar questions about our faith: Do we live with the full power of faith in God, or with only a portion of it while the other part is withering? Statistics indicate that every year millions of people lose or give up their faith in God. How can we meet the challenges of our time, if we lose faith in God and faith in ourselves? The reality of globalization implies that "We've got the whole world on our hands." I ask: Do we really embrace the whole world, if one hand is withered?

Questions can be raised about all aspects of our life. Where? Examine yourself, to see where you might have withered portions of your life, perhaps hidden in your heart, in your thoughts, in your emotions, in your attitudes, in your decisions, in your relations with others. Withered hands not only hinder our serving God in full, but they also hinder us from receiving his blessings in full.

The people we serve are more valuable than the systems in which we function. This is a question of priority. From the mouth of Jesus: "It is lawful to do good on the Sabbath." God's mission is to stretch out the withered hands — our own hands, and the hands of others.

Short silence During the short silence that will follow, reflect on both your good hand and the withered hand, in terms of your personal life, your family, your ministry, and in terms of your responsibility in a global future. Where do we act with one hand? Where do we give with only one hand while withholding back something with the other? Persons are more valuable than sheep. What laws, structures, traditions, prejudices, fears, and habits make us treat people without regard for their dignity and humanness?

Silence . . .

Canticle of Zechariah "Blest be the God of Israel, Who comes to set us free. . . ."

Stretch out your hand "Then Jesus said to the man: 'Stretch out your hand.' And it was restored, was made whole like the other." May we also now stretch out our symbolically withered hands and be free, to follow and serve Jesus as we can.

Prayers
We give thee hearty thanks, O God our Maker and Keeper, for the rest of the past night and for the gift of a new day, with its opportunities of pleasing thee. Grant that we may so pass its hours in freedom, that at eventide we may again give thanks unto thee; through Jesus Christ our Lord.

A morning prayer from the Gelasian Sacramentry: Into thy hands, O Lord, we commend ourselves this day. Let thy presence be with us to its close. Help us to stretch out our hands, to give and to receive. Strengthen us to remember that, in whatsoever good work we do, we are serving thee. Give us a diligent and watchful spirit, that we may seek in all things to know thy will, and knowing it, gladly to perform it, to the honor and glory of thy name; through Jesus Christ our Lord.

Into thy hands, O Lord, we commend ourselves and all who are dear to us this day. Be with us in our going out and in our coming in. Strengthen us for the work which thou hast given us to do. And grant that, filled with thy Holy spirit, we may walk worthy of our high calling, and cheerfully accomplish those things that thou wouldest have done; through Jesus Christ our Lord.

Lord's Prayer

Blessing
Liturgist: To God be honor and glory forever and ever.
People: Amen.
Liturgist: Bless the Lord.
People: The Lord's name be praised.

The people share a sign of peace . . .

*　　　*　　　*

89

REV. PROF. JOHN MBITI

Service of Prayer

Call to worship (Liturgist)
"You are the light of the world. A city set on a hill cannot be hid. Nor do men light a lamp and put it under a bushel, but on a stand, and it gives light to all in the house. Let your light so shine before men, that they may see your good works and give glory to your Father who is in heaven" (Mt 5:14-16).

Hymn "The God of Abraham Praise"

Psalm 67 "God be gracious to us and bless us . . ." responsively (liturgist and congregation).

Prayers (Liturgist)
A prayer of adoration, from St. Augustine: "Great art thou, O Lord, and greatly to be praised. Great is thy power and thy wisdom is infinite. And thee would persons praise . . . persons that bear about them their mortality. Yet would persons praise thee, persons who are but particles of thy creation. Thou awakest us to delight in thy praise. For thou madest us for thyself and our heart is restless until it rests in thee."

Prayer of thanksgiving: From West and East, from North and South you have brought us O Lord, to assemble with one another. We thank you for the challenges that lie before us and for the knowledge and wisdom of your people here gathered. We thank you for the colors of the autumn leaves that fall gently upon the earth; we thank you for the fresh air that we breath; we thank you for the light and warmth of the sun through which you give life on earth. We thank you for the faith handed down through generations from ancient times. Lord, we count it a joy and a privilege, to be called your children, men and women of all ages.

Prayer from Leopold Sedar Senghor, first president of Senegal: The prayer is entitled *The Rainbow of Thy Peace.* "O bless this people, Lord, /Who seek their own face under the mask and can hardly recognize it . . . /O bless this people that breaks its bond . . . /And with them, all the peoples of Europe, /All the peoples of Asia, all the peoples of Oceania, /All the peoples of the Americas and all the peoples of Africa . . . /And see, in the midst of these millions of waves, /The sea swell of the heads of my people. /And grant to their warm hands that they may clasp /The earth in a girdle of brotherly and sisterly hands,/ Beneath the rainbow of thy peace."

Open our ears and grant us attentive minds; instill in us concentrating thoughts, banish from us all prejudice; put us in the position to make creative response, and reward us in the search for answers and new questions, concerning our Faith and Responsibility as one world, one earth. Grant us to laugh with one another, to reflect seriously with one another, to wrestle with our differences and opinions. . . . Equip us all, O Lord, to serve thee and glorify thy holy name, and hear us, as we pray together: Our Father, who is in heaven, hallowed be thy name, thy kingdom come; thy will be done on earth as it is in heaven. Give us this day, our daily bread. Forgive us our debts, as we forgive our debtors. And lead us not into temptation, but deliver us from evil. For thine is the kingdom, the power and the glory. Forever and ever. Amen.

Blessing

The blessing of the God of Abraham, Sarah, and Hagar; and the blessing of the Son born of Mary; and the blessing of the Holy Spirit who watches over us like the mother watches over her baby, be with you now and forever. Amen.

*   *   *

Service of Worship

Call to worship (Liturgist)

"There is a river whose streams make glad the city of God, the holy habitation of the Most High. God is in the midst of her, she shall not be moved. God will help her right early. . . . 'Be still, and know that I am God. I am exalted among the nations, I am exalted in the earth!' The Lord of hosts is with us, the God of Jacob is our refuge" (Ps 46:4-7, 10, 11).

Let us stand up and continue our service:

LITURGIST: O, Lord, open my lips.
PEOPLE: And my mouth shall proclaim your praise.
LITURGIST: The Lord's unfailing love and mercy never cease.
PEOPLE: Fresh as the morning and sure as the sunrise.

Psalm 100: The cantor sings the verses and we all sing the refrain.
(Make a joyful noise to the Lord . . .) "Arise, come to your God, singing your songs of rejoicing."

Scripture Reading Luke 24:13ff.
Liturgist: The Word of the Lord.
People: Thanks be to God.

Meditation

What a great passage, that we have just heard! It is rich in meaning, in
nourishment. It can engage us the whole morning. However, we take
two thoughts for our meditation.

One thought has to do with faith. Two men are going from Jerusalem to Emmaus in the countryside. Being the spiritual center of the people of Israel, Jerusalem nourishes the rest of the country. Technically
speaking, the two men should be taking with them the warmth and joy,
the hope and heart of Israel as represented by the great temple in Jerusalem. Millions of pilgrims came from afar to pay their spiritual homage
here. Jerusalem is the spiritual keeper and citadel of Israel.

Being followers of Jesus, who have personal knowledge of him, the
two men should be traveling from Jerusalem with a double message: to
tell about Jerusalem and the feast of the Passover, which they have attended. In addition, they should tell about the great and hot news of the
resurrection of Jesus, which they have heard in the course of the day.
The resurrection of Jesus was still hot news, exciting news, headline
news, unique news.

But, this is not the case with the two men. They avoid the most important news, and instead they become messengers of unbelief and dis-
appointment. They spread it in an intricate way. "We had hoped that he
was the one to redeem Israel. . . ." Such a statement implies clearly that
they were mistaken in their hope. They had shared the hope of Israel.
Now, they no longer hold such a hope. It has vanished.

Touching on the resurrection they are even more elusive: "Some women of our company *amazed us*. They were at the tomb early in the morning and did not find his body; and they came back saying that they had *even seen a vision of angels*, who said that he was alive. . . .'" What a sound academic reshuffling of ideas, clearly avoiding any commitment. "Some of our company amazed us": here the two men detach themselves from telling directly the news of the resurrection, which they don't believe. Therefore, they put it vaguely, that it is "some of our company" who are spreading this (for them) questionable information. The two do not include themselves in the verification or reliability of that news. In a very patriarchal society, such a story can only be attributed to women! And even then, they rationalize the report of the women, by saying that the women had seen a *vision of angels*.

The two continue to spread their unbelief. They tell it to the stranger who happens to be walking with them. We read: "Jesus himself drew near and went with them. But their eyes were kept from recognizing him." This is both reassuring and frightening. It is reassuring to know that Jesus keeps his followers company, not only because of our faith in him but also in spite of lack of it. Jesus walking with us, with you and me through all the paths of life.

That is wonderful. But it is also frightening: "Their eyes were kept from recognizing him." Generally, people who live in the countryside tend to know everyone else around them. As I grew up in the countryside in Kenya, I came to know the majority of people within a radius of five miles (eight kilometers). You simply learnt to recognize other people through the gait of their walking, the sound of their voice and coughing, and their footprints on the unpaved footpaths, their cattle in the fields, etc. Everyone recognized everyone else.

In our story, the two men walk seven miles (eleven kilometers) with Jesus, but fail to recognize him, their friend. They address him as a stranger, as a visitor: "Are you the only visitor to Jerusalem, who does not know the things that have happened there these days?" they ask Jesus in great astonishment, rebukingly. It is incredible, that one fails to recognize a friend who died only three days before. This is frightening, if you grow up in a religious family or country and go the whole way of life speaking about Jesus but being unable to recognize him when he walks

93

with you. To call him a stranger, a visitor, is not enough. You lose the minutes, the hours, the phases and chapters in your life-story, in which you edge out Jesus, turning him into a visitor in Jerusalem, who does not even know about his own events. Some of our theological scholarship seems to know him better than he knows himself!

An African story is told about a man and his star wife. Like many other people, the man kept cattle as his mainstay. Every day he drove the cattle to the fields to feed them, to graze them and bring them back home in the evening. The next morning he would get up and milk them before taking them out again. But suddenly, when in the morning he went to get milk, he would find the udders floppy and empty, having no milk. This went on day after day. He got very concerned. He could not understand it.

One day he decided to keep watch at night and see what was happening to his cattle when he went to sleep. Around midnight, he saw a string or rope stretching from the sky to the ground. Descending on rope there came down from the stars a group of beautiful women, each carrying a basket. They went to the cows, milked them, and then returned to the sky. The man knew why he was getting no milk from his cows. He waited again another night, and as usual the women came down and started to milk his cows. He jumped out and surprised them, and managed to capture one of the women before the rest could climb back to the sky. He kept her as his wife.

The star woman had a basket with her. It had a lid. She told the man that he must never look into that basket. He never looked into it. They lived happily for many years. As time went on, he became curious about the basket. So, one day, while the wife was out of the house, the man went and lifted the lid of the basket and looked inside. He saw nothing. He laughed very much about the empty basket.

The wife came home and asked the husband if he had looked into the basket. He said yes, and laughed, telling her that there was nothing inside. The woman packed her things and said to the man: "I will leave you now, not because you looked into my basket, but because you saw nothing in it." She left him and never returned.

Jesus has been walking with the world, for more than ten miles, for two thousand years. His followers have talked again and again about him; millions upon millions have preached about him. Volumes and volumes of books have written about him on parchment, on papyrus, on paper, on wood, on stone, on the computer screen. . . . I ask myself, which part of this two-thousand-year history still speaks of him as "stranger," "visitor," and fails to recognize him. What kept the eyes of the two disciples from recognizing him? Was it not their unbelief? "O foolish men, and slow of heart to believe"; Jesus brought them to their senses with this hard word. Slowness to believe — that was their problem. Is it perhaps also our problem today?

Short silent meditation
For our short period of silent meditation, we may pose questions such as: Do I fail to recognize Jesus my Lord, who walks with me every day, because I am slow to believe? Do I recognize him, when he turns up in the library where I am occupied doing my reading? Do I recognize him on the street when I am walking to catch the train? Do I recognize him on the computer screen, in the face of babies, in the beauty of the flowers, in my fellow traveler, in the scriptures that have been translated into more than 2,200 languages?

Silence . . .

Canticle of Zechariah: "Blest be the God of Israel, who comes to set us free. . . ."

Prayers
We shall use three prayers: a traditional morning prayer from the Oromo people of Ethiopia; a prayer for our meetings, from the Samburu people of Kenya; and a Jewish prayer for increase of faith in order to find God. We close the prayers with our Lord's own prayer.

For the new day: O God, you have prepared in peace the path we must follow today. Help us to walk straight on that path. If we speak, remove lies from our lips. If we are hungry, take away from us all complaint (and give us enough to eat and drink). If we have plenty, destroy pride in us. May we go through the day calling on you, you O Lord, who know no other Lord ("Oromo," in A. J. Gittins, ed., *Heart of Prayer* [London, 1985], p. 28).

95

For meetings: "Our God, who are in all things, rise up from the abyss. Our God, enable us to agree both in the morning and in the evening. Our God, breathe upon us with your blessed breath, and, our God, answer what we have said. And God said: 'All right'" (Samburu, Kenya, from Gittins, ed., *Heart of Prayer,* p. 132).

For faith to recognize God: Creator: where shall I find you? High and hidden is your place. And where shall I not find you? The world is full of your glory. I have sought your nearness, with all my heart, I called you, and going out to meet you, I found you coming to meet me (*Judah Halevi,* p. 68).

Lord Jesus, take away from us the blindness of little faith, of unbelief, and grant that we may recognize you as you walk with us from Jerusalem to Emmaus. We rejoice to know that you walk with us, on both the smooth and rocky paths, in the morning, afternoon, and evening of our life. We thank you.

As you taught us, so we are bold to pray together: Our Father in heaven, hallowed be your name. Your kingdom come. Your will be done, on earth as in heaven. Give us today our daily bread. Forgive us our sins as we forgive those who sin against us. Save us from the time of trial and deliver us from evil. For the kingdom, the power, and the glory are yours now and forever. Amen.

Blessing
Liturgist: To God be honor and glory forever and ever.
People: Amen.
Liturgist: Bless the Lord.
People: The Lord's name be praised.
The people share a sign of peace . . .

III

THE SPIRIT, WHOLENESS, AND HEALTH

Introduction

In our churches we worship the God who never changes, the One who is the Alpha and Omega, who knows all things, created all things, and redeems all things. Yet outside their walls, we encounter unprecedented changes, unceasing demands which seemingly have no beginning or end, a world where some know far more than others, and where the fruit of human creativity dominates our existence. The press of change in our technological world so controls our daily lives that it's easy to be tempted to believe that the God of Abraham, Isaac, and Jacob, the sandal-clad redeemer who strode the dusty paths of Galilee, at best doesn't understand and at worst is irrelevant in our contemporary world. Human creativity seems more determinative than God's creativity, people seem more sovereign than the Savior, and material things more valued than spiritual truths.

As we enter the new millennium, never before in history has the development of a theology of technology been more imperative. Without a clear understanding of the role of human creativity in God's creative purposes, without means for evaluating and valuing the worth and desirability of things, our lives will be more controlled by our desires than by God's design. Only with an appropriate theology of technology can we steward properly God's creation and the fruit of our own creativity.

Tragically, the church has often been theologically impoverished. Pastors and church leaders are equipped with a theology of sin and salvation, of the Trinity and eschatology. Who has the tools to think theologically about computer chips and cyberspace, and gene therapy and Prozac, or even about fishing and recycling? To lead the church into our globalized future, church leaders need to expand the subject matter in their systematic study of theology.

Without this, we risk having our lives led by our things rather than by our faith, and will tend to worship and serve the human creation rather than the divine Creator. In so doing we will risk destroying creation and the quality of our human community along with it, rather than guarding and protecting them.

In the first essay on "Science, Technology, and Mission," Ronald Cole-Turner issues a compelling call for the evangelization of technology. How many church mission programs think of computer science and bioengineering projects as suitable domains for Christian mission? How many churches commission on a Sunday morning all their members who work professionally in the development of new technologies? We prayerfully send forth our high school youth groups to volunteer for a week in urban slums — and well we should. We lay hands on elders and Sunday school teachers, setting them apart for their ministry in our parish — and well we should. However, Cole-Turner warns us that our technological innovations are not merely remaking our environment, they are remaking human nature itself. More than merely issuing a warning, Cole-Turner concludes with four recommendations that should guide every church's ministry as we seek to steward and control, rather than be controlled by, the fruit of human hands.

If we're impoverished by the absence of a theology of technology, so does all of creation suffer from our lack of a theology of the environment. Susan Power Bratton calls for the development of "econormative" ethics, the focus of Christian ministry on global ecological change. Using the case of global fisheries, fish resource depletion, and cultivation as case study, she develops an intricate analysis and set of guidelines to inform the church's engagement in ecological stewardship. Rather than merely pitting human economic well-being and creation care against each other as foes, she provides insights into how the good of both natural resources and human communities can be secured. She concludes by offering valuable suggestions for ways Christian institutions can enter into the ministry of ecology.

The final article in this section provides a compelling analysis of modern, Western medicine. Allen Verhey questions from a global perspective some of the presuppositions of our contemporary approaches to health care. Lacking an appropriate theology of medicine, the church has tended to adopt the values and goals of the health care industry. Through the parable of the Good Samaritan, Verhey calls for a return to compassion and to confidence in the Spirit of God as underlying values characterizing our approach to medicine. From this perspective he offers provocative proposals for health care policies and priorities.

These three articles can not only help church leaders and theologians pursue new areas of theological inquiry. They can also affirm and empower laypersons in their ministries, people who may have previously believed that ministry was confined to "church work." In so doing, the church can be propelled into vital avenues of mission, and the world will discover more fully the wonder of the grace of God.

Tim Dearborn

7

Science, Technology, and Mission

RONALD COLE-TURNER

Of all the forms of change we face today, those that spring from technology are the most radically determinative of our future, for they drive economic, political, and cultural changes forward at an ever-increasing speed. In the twenty-first century, we will enter an era in which we will acquire unprecedented technological power to define and alter our selves.

Technology's reach is unbounded, affecting everything from how we make war or love or art or wealth. And when we feel we cannot cope with it anymore we use technology yet again to control our brains, altering their function and so regulating our mood and our personality. There is no place to hide from technology, no inner sanctuary of the self left unmanipulated, no part of creation untouched.

Technology's allure is captivating, mesmerizing us with the latest gadgetry. Technology stocks make their initial public offerings on the Internet and digitized capital follows instantly, blindly, voraciously, energizing economies while widening gaps between poor and rich, between the savvy and the sidelined.

Technology's new powers explode so quickly that few of us comprehend their full significance. Who can possibly understand today's technology? Who can keep up? Even experts are blindsided when technology leaps ahead unexpectedly. Startled, we wonder, *What does this mean? How can this be good? What problem will this solve, and what problems will it create? Where will it all end? Can anyone control it?*

Can theology — that communal process by which the church's faith seeks to understand — can theology aim at understanding technology? Can we put the words *God* and *technology* together in any kind of meaningful sentence? Can theology guess what God is doing in today's technology? Or by our silence do we leave it utterly godless? Can we have a theology of technology that comprehends, gives meaning to, dares to influence the direction and set limits to this explosion of new powers?

The greatest danger of technology lies not in its rapidly expanding powers or even its deliberate use for evil purposes, but in the fact that it moves blindly forward in a vacuum of critical reflection. We use it. It transforms us. And we do not think about it. We are the guinea pigs of our own experiments, engineers now engineered, caught in a mindless blizzard of our own novelty-making. We are remaking human nature without so much as a serious discussion or a self-critical pause. The only limit is ingenuity, the only guidance is the market, and the only end is more.

As never before, the world needs the church. The challenge before us is nothing less than to *evangelize* this new reality, this peculiar phenomenon of late modernity, this technological transformation of humanity. Can technology's transformations themselves be transformed by Christ? Can we human beings, reordered by the power of Christ, gain some capacity to stand in critical judgment of our technological pretensions and self-delusions? Dare we hope that through the church and its mission, Christ can reorder technology itself as an instrument in the service of healing, compassion, and justice?

Such hope seems entirely unrealistic, not so much because of the magnitude of the problem but because of the lack of readiness on the part of the church. The church is scarcely aware of the momentous advances in human genetics or neuroscience or the Internet that have occurred in the past decade. Church leaders barely use desktop computers, and clergy seem intimidated by science, medicine, and technology.

But then we must remember that scientists, physicians, and engineers of every type are in the church. Their insight, seldom used, is an asset of enormous value. Theological schools, in spite of their longstanding advice to entering students not to major in science or technology, suddenly find themselves overwhelmed with second career students

101

who bring high levels of technical skill and knowledge into the seminary classroom. Today's clergy, though they may be barely aware of science and technology, know that they preach to people who possess high levels of skill in these areas. Increasingly, today's clergy are recognizing that theology is a task of the whole people of God, best done when informed by the experiences and insights of the whole community.

The church will need all these resources if it is to take up its mission in and to a technological world. In order to engage effectively in mission, it must first learn the language and the culture. Only then can we arrive at a theological understanding of technology and of its transformative powers, taking into account its cultural, commercial, global, and quasi-religious dimensions.

Technology is the power to bend nature to our desires. And as an ever-expanding power, technology rivals traditional patterns of human behavior and traditional forms of human dependence, tempting us to abandon any remaining trust we may have in a diminished version of God and to trust instead in the omnipotence of our own techniques. Each time technology advances, our need for God shrinks.

In such a context, the church is confronted with two urgent tasks. The first is theology and science, a task of interpretation whereby theology draws upon science in order to illumine its understanding of divine creativity. Fortunately, theologians have recently begun to take up this task. The second is theology of technology, which seeks to understand the raw frenzy of human creativity, daring to comprehend it and claim it as a new mode of God's action, offered to the glory of God and in the service of God. Regrettably, theologians have largely neglected this second task.

By engaging in a *theology of technology*, the church struggles to be faithful to the God who, like technology itself, makes all things new. How are we to relate God's novelty-making to our own? What connection is there between God's transformation of all things and our transformation of almost everything? Are these rival processes? As a matter of fact, many do see technology as "playing God," as the proud intrusion of human will into the business of ordering and shaping nature. Technology is reliable, efficient, trustworthy, and offers us such control that a Faustian bargain seems the only logical precondition. Technology's challenge to theology is this: Can theology bring technology's potentially rival powers into the service of God? Can theology help us recognize technology as God's instrument?

This task is more urgent today than ever before in the history of the church. Our mission is not merely in and to the world, but in and to all the forces which impinge upon it and which make it what it will be. The magnitude of change from technology in the twenty-first century will be staggering, vastly outstripping the magnitude of change that occurred in the twentieth. But more important than the sheer amount of change is the quality of the changes. It is not simply more of the same, and we cannot hope to comprehend it by analogy with the past.

Past technologies altered our environment; the new technologies will alter our souls. In past technologies, we human beings acted on what was around us, and in small ways through medical technology we acted on our own bodies. But we acted as if we who did the engineering were not part of the nature we engineered, as if a functional dualism protected our selves from our effects. The new technology slashes through any such functional dualism and alters the agent.

Already we can see this with psychopharmacology, prescription drugs sold under trade names such as Prozac or Ritalin. Prozac, for instance, was carefully designed to exploit new understandings of the human brain and of the role of a key neurotransmitter, serotonin. By affecting this neurotransmitter, Prozac affects the mood, lifting many from depression and anxiety to a more hopeful outlook. Ritalin, which is widely prescribed for children with attention deficit disorder, helps them focus, pay attention, and finish what they intend to do. In both cases, the effect is on the self, the core of the personality, the will, or what theology used to call the soul.

This is just the beginning. Far more powerful technologies are now being developed, foretelling a new era of unprecedented human control over human beings. Be assured, the justification for these new technologies is therapy, not control. And their capacity for therapy, for relief of suffering or from the limitations of disease and injury, will be enormous. But the technologies of therapy are inseparable from the technologies of control, of enhancement, of personal aggrandizement in the face of increasingly competitive pressures to win against our technologically enhanced rivals. Ahead lies not just steroids for athletes but broad-based technological enhancement for competitive performance in all realms of human endeavor, including mental activity.

Of one thing we can be sure: Unguided, uncomprehended, and uncriticized, these technologies of therapy will inevitably become technologies of control, driven by competitive frenzies. So utterly do we modern human beings lack anything resembling control of our technology that only the most naive dare to hope it can be steered. The irony, though sad, should not be overlooked: for in seeking control through technology, we have lost or are about to lose the very thing we seek. We can control the details with laser-like precision, but can we any longer control the whole, this rampant profusion of powers? More fundamentally, can we control our own use even individually, much less collectively?

Consider what lies ahead in genetics. The Human Genome Project is almost completed, offering us complete knowledge of human DNA and the ability to understand how it functions. Genetic sequences that can be described can be altered, even when they are in cells inside the human body. We are learning to treat genetic diseases not just by trying to counter their symptoms but by attacking their cause at the genetic level. As we pass the year 2000, this strategy of "gene therapy" will cease to be experimental, and will be applied not just to genetic diseases like cystic fibrosis but to a host of diseases, such as cancer, because genes play some role in all disease.

The next step in the advance of this technology is very likely to be the genetic treatment of fetuses before birth. Some genetic diseases cause irreversible damage before birth, and so to be successful any treatment must occur before then. In 1999, the United States National Institutes of Health convened a major conference to discuss the feasibility and the ethics of prenatal, *in utero* gene therapy. Such an attempt appears to be less than a decade away. One of the concerns posed by treating a fetus is that the treatment will pass to the sex cells of the fetus and from there to future generations. Inheritable genetic modifications (usually called human germ line modifications) have generally been opposed, partly for reasons of technical safety but also because of more fundamental ethical reasons, such as our limited right to treat future patients without their consent.

In the case of fetal gene therapy, the primary intention would be to benefit the fetus, not to alter its offspring. Any inheritable modification would be unintended. But since unintended modification cannot be ruled out, the debate currently in the United States is whether such fetal therapy should be permitted if it might unintentionally cause inheritable modifications. It is quite likely, in my opinion, that permission will be given for this technique. And if that occurs, it is also likely, not too many years in the future, that we will permit *intentional* inheritable genetic modifications for the prevention of disease. The attraction will be very strong. Imagine preventing Tay Sachs or sickle cell, not just in the next generation, but in all future generations.

As these technologies are being developed, we are simultaneously coming to new insight into the role that genes play, not just in disease, but in predispositions to behavior and to traits of personality. This area of study, referred to as behavior genetics, has begun to attain surprising clarity in some of its findings. In the past few years, geneticists have found relationships between specific gene sequences and core behavioral traits or predispositions to patterns of behavior, ranging from aggressiveness to anxiety. Studies are underway to link genes to addictive behaviors, intelligence, and sexual orientation, as well as many other traits or predispositions.

Through these studies, we will very likely gain a new and highly detailed picture of how our genes help to define the very core of our identity. This of course will have profound theological implications, especially because we will have to confront the theological significance of genetic differences among human beings at the level of personality and predisposition. Based on what we know now, we should expect to learn that genes alone do not define us or our traits, but that genes must be seen as interacting with environmental factors in incredibly complex ways. Traits and predispositions, not to mention specific behaviors, are the result of these interactions and never the result of genes alone. However, we can already see a shift in popular culture toward genetic interpretations of human nature, often tending toward genetic determinism. One role for theology will be to counter this excessive determinism.

Nevertheless, we must remember that it is precisely in a highly competitive culture, which exaggerates the determinative power of genes, that these new technologies are arriving daily and being pressed into service. Already today, some parents are selecting among embryos in order to avoid genetic disease. That same technology, wedded to only slightly more advanced behavior genetics, could provide a plausible basis for behavioral selection. And so if we can glimpse a bit further into the future, but not too many years away, it is not at all too far-fetched to imagine parents selecting embryos based on the predictions of behavioral genetics or based on other desirable traits, such as height, that have nothing to do with avoiding disease. In that way, technologies developed for therapy will be used for control, competition, and enhancement.

The next stage will be intentional germ line alteration, probably ten to twenty years in the future. This is more than cloning, for cloning merely replicates what is given, while germ line alteration brings with it the ability to improve upon what is there. The technology is complex and nowhere close to being safe for human use, although success with animals has been achieved, and research will proceed rapidly. Through any number of possible techniques, children will be brought into the world with genes that are not merely *chosen* before birth but modified by adding new genes or deleting undesirable genes. These changes will be present in all the resulting cells of the body and passed on to offspring. With this step, we will produce what are often called "designer babies." Technologies first developed to make babies well will be used to make them better.

And not just babies. These emerging technologies will be powerfully effective in treating diseases and in forestalling the aging process. In late 1998, researchers succeeded in isolating human embryonic stem cells and in producing a self-sustaining culture of such cells. These have the potential to become nearly any kind of cell in the body, and the hope is that they will provide unlimited supplies of cells and tissues for implantation into the human body at the site of disease or injury. Damaged cells and tissues might simply be replaced. Using cloning technology combined with stem cell technology, medicine in the future could create implantable cells or tissues that are genetically identical to the host, or even alter them genetically to make them better than the cells that were damaged. These implants could work in many areas of the human body, reversing injury or disease. In 1998, the first clinical trials of brain cell implants began in the United States. The hope is that these implanted cells will be incorporated into the structure and functions of the brain, leading eventually to an effective repair for the damage caused by strokes, Parkinson's, or Alzheimer's disease.

Longer life spans, greater mental ability, resistance to various diseases. . . . How far will this go? Consider the projections of one prominent scientist, Lee Silver. Referring to a time about two centuries from now, Silver comments: "It was a critical turning point in the evolution of life in the universe. . . . Throughout it all, there were those who said we couldn't go any further, that there were limits to mental capacity and technological advances. But those prophesied limits were swept aside, one after another, as intelligence, knowledge, and technological power continued to rise" (Silver, 1998, p. 292). Silver continues, referring now to a time more than a millennium away: "A special point has now been reached in the distant future. And in this era, there exists a special group of mental beings. Although these beings can trace their ancestry back directly to *homo sapiens*, they are as different from humans as humans are from the primitive worms with tiny brains that first crawled along the earth's surface" (Silver, 1998, pp. 292-93). Silver believes we will engineer our own replacement, the *trans-human*. How far *will* this go?

And of course, genetics and medicine are not the only areas of rapid advance in technology. Equally rapid and portentous advances are occurring in computer technology and communications. Overwhelmingly, the far greater part of the digital revolution lies ahead. And here is a technology, unlike genetics, that the church itself will use in its own life and work as the church, and by using be transformed.

Very likely, computers and the Internet will create new horizontal ecclesiastical structures that will overlay traditional vertical structures, such as denominations, or local associations, such as local ecumenical councils. Alongside these will rise new linkages built upon digitized networks and electronic pathways. These new forms of non-local structure will follow special concerns or forms of mission rather than geography or denomination, and they will permit heightened levels of interactivity and mutuality. At the same time, denominations might experience new strength and vitality as they attain an increased ability to link local congregations into a truly connectional or organic reality, capable of subtle feedback loops and heightened self-awareness.

Congregations will continue to gather for worship, of course, and various hands-on forms of Christian service will go on largely unchanged. But even here, indirectly, the persons engaging in ministry will themselves be profoundly different. We will be deeply changed by *"Life on the Screen,"* to borrow a phrase from the title of a book by Sherry Turkle, even if we can now only dimly foresee the contours of that change (Turkle, 1995). Many of us already spend more time in front of the screen than we do in front of people.

Churches need to be prepared for the wide impact of the digital revolution, as computer chips proliferate and drop in price so dramatically that they are used once and thrown away. People will communicate routinely with one another through the Internet, not by typing e-mail but by audio/video linkage that realistically duplicates face-to-face contact. Business, education, medicine, and nearly every other aspect of life will be reorganized as distance ceases to be a barrier to human interaction.

But of all the prospects that lie ahead in the digital revolution, perhaps the most perplexing are those that join digital and genetic or biological technologies. For example, as we enter the twenty-first century, we are being greeted by the "gene chip," a hybrid technology that marries genetics with data processing, so that gene sequences can be read automatically, almost instantly. Actual DNA sequences are embedded in a chip. A test sample of DNA is applied to the embedded sample, and similarities and differences are immediately revealed in computer-enhanced images on a screen. The value for diagnostic medicine can hardly be underestimated, especially in the future as pharmaceutical companies develop drugs that are increasingly individualized to fit the genetic characteristics of individual patients. Soon, our health future will be predicted, not by a crystal ball but by DNA in silicon. This technology is already on the market, and it allows the user to construct specific gene tests, for a disease-related sequence or for personal identification purposes, and then quickly test individuals, cheaply and automatically.

A more dramatic example of the merging of silicon and biological technologies lies in the area of brain implants that are highly miniaturized computers or computer interfaces. In the late 1990s, the first experiments were conducted. Attempts to restore sight to the blind by feeding electrical impulses directly from video cameras into the visual cortex of the brain have met with some early success, as have similar efforts to restore hearing. Patients who were unable to use their limbs were implanted, in the motor cortex of their brains, with special devices designed to serve as an interface between the brain's electrochemical activity and a computer's digital electronics. The device contained microscopic electrodes seeded with neural growth factor, a natural chemical that induces brain growth. Living cells in the patients' brains grow toward these tiny electrodes so that the electrodes can detect the brain's activity and turn it into computer input data. As of 1999, one paralyzed patient was able to think of moving a part of his body, and by doing so to move a cursor on a computer screen. In this way he could give the computer simple instructions, without any form of communication except brain activity.

Where might this lead? Few of us are troubled by the idea of using technology to help people with injuries regain their normal functions. But such devices implanted in people without illness or injury, merely as a way of enhancing their powers, is another question altogether. It will very likely become possible to provide enhanced data perception, enabling such things as infrared vision, perhaps first for soldiers or police. Someday it might be possible to implant chips that carry enormous amounts of stored data, virtual libraries, whose contents could then be recalled in an instant, as if they were part of the natural memory. Surely this will pose troubling questions of the self, its identity, its memories, and the integrity of its own experience, and some day persons with implants may no longer recognize the boundaries of their "true" self. Even more troubling is the possibility that the wiring could be reversed: Instead of using the brain to control the computer, use the computer to control the brain. It would be profoundly troubling to contemplate a person with an implant whose experiences or moods are under the control of another person.

The potential for therapy is enormous, but so is the likelihood of great misuse. It seems almost inevitable that these technologies will be used in ways that are morally degrading *and* morally uplifting, for great evil *and* great good. And it is impossible to bundle up the bad technologies and lock them away while leaving the good technologies available for use. Every technique that we have considered will always have multiple possibilities. It is altogether likely that these technologies will be used in an intensely competitive environment for projects of self-enhancement and for the enhancement and control of our offspring. When this happens, we will take from our offspring some of the freedom that comes from the unpredictability of procreation and replace it with some of the control that accompanies their having been designed.

There is, I believe, no way to stop this technology or entirely to prevent such enhancement and control of offspring from happening. What then is the role of the church? What is our mission in this emerging twenty-first-century technological culture? Can we step forward as the church into the public arena and share the moral burden of public deliberation about technology's development and use, thereby altering our broad cultural response to technology and thus helping to steer this careening vehicle we have built but have not yet learned to drive? But if we had the influence, toward what end would we steer? And by what means, with what mechanisms of engagement? How can *this* church engage *this* culture? There are four proposals I wish to make. Separately they offer little basis for hope. But taken together, they may solidify the church in mission to make a real difference in the shape and structure of the future.

First, the church should intentionally become a public space for deliberation, criticism, cultural comprehension of technology in all of its manifestations, powers, impotencies, promises, and dangers. Per Anderson has written about the need in our pervasively pro-technology culture for an open and critical forum, a public space where technology is challenged and cross-examined. Where might this happen, if not in the church? Anderson challenges us "to enable the religious communities to be counter-cultural spaces for forming critical consciousness and social responsibility about science and technology. . . . Do the established institutions of science and technology need some kind of 'loyal opposition,' a cool, critical gaze from a different viewpoint, a different understanding of what it means to 'live well'?" (Anderson, 1998, pp. 4-5). By creating an open space for discussion, education, critical reflection on culture and on ourselves, the church would bestow a gift of enormous value upon a society that almost entirely lacks such a space.

Second, through proclamation, teaching, and community formation, the church should cultivate an ethic of appropriate use of technology. Our critical standard for technology is this: Technology should improve health and human flourishing in environmentally sustainable

110

ways and contribute to greater social justice. To the extent it fails, we withhold support. For instance, human reproductive technology might be defensible as contributing to the flourishing of couples in their desire to become parents, but it might fail in regard to their spending tens of thousands of dollars to have a child "of their own" in a world where hundreds of millions of children suffer from malnutrition, and so our support of such technologies needs to be sharply critical. Above all, the church should cultivate resistance to the prevailing culture of frenzied, competitively driven, and controlling uses. We must be communities of resistance to the use of technology to define, control, or design our offspring to fit the specifications of a competitive society, and we must cultivate an ethic of unconditional acceptance even while we point our children to their true destiny to enjoy the fellowship God offers.

Third, the church should form the faith and vocation of Christian scientists and engineers and should lift up these vocations for young people as an appropriate way to live out one's faith. Too often in our church, science and technology are ignored or only criticized, creating the impression that it is an intrinsically anti-Christian career and that young people who pursue it should leave the church. And in addition to everything else the church loses when they leave, we lose the opportunity to form the religious consciousness and moral character of tomorrow's scientists and engineers. More than any other sector of society, the religious institutions have the power to shape how scientists and engineers frame the meaning of their work and the purpose it serves.

Fourth, the church in a technological age must cultivate a practical awareness of a theology of technology. Through proclamation, teaching, and worship, the church must frame technology with prayer, by which we offer ourselves and our technology in gratitude and worship. Technology may be created in our laboratories, but in church we place it in the hands of God as an instrument of God's action, rightly used to the extent that it achieves God's purposes but wrongly used when it contradicts them. In worship we dare to imagine God using our technology, and in so doing we redefine its powers as subservient to Christ. We dare to recognize, in our own human discoveries, what God is making possible. And we dare to ask how God can transform the powers that form the future.

Works Cited

Anderson, Per. "Cultivating the Cool, Critical Gaze: On Saying 'No' to 'Dolly' and the Future of the Faith-Science Dialogue," *Covalence: The Bulletin of the Ecumenical Roundtable on Science, Technology, and the Church* 1, no. 3-4 (May-August,1998): 4-5.

Silver, Lee. *Remaking Eden: How Genetic Engineering and Cloning Will Transform the American Family.* New York: Avon, 1998.

Turkle, Sherry. *Life on the Screen: Identity in the Age of the Internet.* New York: Simon and Schuster, 1995.

8

Christian Response to Changes in Global Ecosystems

SUSAN POWER BRATTON

Globalization of Ecological Trends

Until recently, the majority of Christian ethicists and theologians ignored the plethora of planet-wide issues documented in a diverse and dispersed international environmental science and policy literature. The field seemed eclectic — muddled by jargon and esoteric models of the planet in the year 2050. Environmental activism was, after all, fostered by social malcontents and political radicals. However, Christians who believe we have responsibilities to the hungry and thirsty, the poor and marginalized, can hardly turn their faces away from changes in the earth's habitats that cause food or water shortages. Nor can we ignore environmental deterioration that may threaten the health and well-being of our own children and grandchildren. Whatever the future, some forms of global environmental change are already well underway and are testing humanity's ability to sustain its own ever-growing population (Bratton, 1992).

Although Christian ethicists have recently argued about the legitimacy of some global ecological concerns, such as climate change (Derr and Nash, 1996), I will present a global ecological issue that is not scientifically contested and use it to stimulate Christian ethical response. Business records, loss of small fishing ports, economic displacement of fishers, and scientific surveys of marine organisms all verify deteriora-

113

tion of key ocean resources. Not just vulnerable freshwater or near-shore marine fisheries have declined, but numerous open ocean fish populations have fallen below "sustainable harvest." Pollution and eco-system degradation are widespread in all the planet's oceans.

Open ocean harvests are presently dominated by the "distant water fishing nations" who may move thousands of miles to locate the most productive fishing grounds. If fish populations are depleted in one re-gion, the fleets simply move to another. A recent summary of threats to marine food resources by Alain Le Sann (1998) points to the spread of globalization and the role of multinational fishing companies as critical concerns, as is the deployment of commercial fish harvests to pay Third World debt. The "South" is increasing its fishing and is an "exporter"; while the "North" continues to be a major importer, and is caught in a morass of quotas and mismanagement. Global fishing fleets are over-capitalized, while post-harvest losses of fish remain high. The coastal ecosystems that produce fish, including mangrove swamps and marshes (critical nurseries for fish and shellfish) are being degraded and de-stroyed.

The politics of fishing have changed greatly as fleets have industri-alized and globalized their harvest strategies. Consolidated economic in-terests, such as the European Union, have created large, well-organized markets. Nations are now invoking Exclusive Economic Zones stretch-ing two hundred nautical miles out to sea. Environmental groups are an increasing force in maritime politics, while environmental protection laws may have both positive and negative impacts, such as inhibiting trade. While regulations have tightened and now favor transferable quo-tas, conflicts are erupting more and more frequently, between vessels and among national fleets. Le Sann (1998) reports that "in most Asian and African countries, fish is a major food item, representing respec-tively, 29 percent and 25 percent of the supply of animal protein in local diets." In 40 countries (39 in the South), fish are "the principal source of protein." Le Sann (1998) summarizes: "Unfortunately, in the poorest countries, domestic consumption of marine produce is often hampered by a bias towards exports of fish products from South to North, as well as by demographic growth."

So where, in this complex tangle of international relations, does Christianity fit?

Whither Christian Response?

One of the bad habits of Christian ethical response to global ecological trends is to repeatedly argue whether ecological issues are worthy of ethical discussion or not, and never progress to developing concrete programs of action. A second inadequate tactic is to call for environmental action, or to back what the major environmental advocacy organizations are proclaiming and go no further. Too often Christians simply repeat the summations of academic ecologists or policy experts, and don't convey their message as well, or as convincingly as they do. I would like to petition for *econormative ethics* intended to focus Christian ministry on the elements of global ecological change Christianity is best adapted to handle, or has a specific biblical mandate (or calling) to engage.

Econormative ethics assumes that our responses to global ecological change include virtues, attitudes, and duties, which must be incorporated at all levels of social organization — from the family to the United Nations. Environmental ethics has to be compatible with other ethical concerns of a specific social entity or community in order to be both accepted and implemented.

Both environmental activists and Christian ecotheologians prefer to present environmental values as an umbrella casting shade on the rest of our lives. The emphasis is on abstractions such as the inherent value of the nonhuman cosmos or on universal theological concepts such as God's role as Creator. There is nothing wrong with an astute reading of Genesis 1 or Psalm 104, but such exegesis is not, by its self, adequate to help resolve problems originating somewhere between folk fishers off the Ivory Coast and international fleets flying the flags of France and Japan. Our actual environmental ethic is imbedded in our rules for keeping a household (the subject of extensive New Testament commentary), the principles of our trade or profession, our means of developing community infrastructure (such as water systems or highways), our pursuit of education and lifestyle (including entertainment and recreation), and our national agendas in sharing the atmosphere and oceans with other sovereign states.

Econormative ethics is based on the concept that an effective environmental ethos must be compatible and integrated with a community's overall ethical priorities. To this end, Christians should:

1. Determine the present role of Christianity in determining the ethical responses of fishing communities. What influence does Christianity have now, if any?

2. Understand the ethical priorities of fishers, including their concerns for issues such as safely operating vessels and nets, or their responsibilities for feeding their families. (Econormative study asks questions such as: What are the ethical priorities of the fishers? Which virtues, values, and duties are the most important? Are environmental values or virtues expressed, and if so, are they a primary or secondary priority? What sorts of language are used to express virtues, duties, and social norms? How do the fishers perceive their relationship to the marine environment? Do they utilize aesthetic, religious, or scientific language to describe the sea? Are community ethics equally robust at all levels of social organization?)

3. Understand the specific sources of ethical and societal dysfunction that result in ocean degradation and fisheries collapse. Is it really weak environmental values, or do the problems lie elsewhere? Is it likely that fishers are exceptionally greedy? Why, in social terms, is overexploitation so common?

4. Evaluate the social circumstances and communities where Christian ministry or intervention could be the most helpful. In the fisheries case, are we ignoring the needs of other Christians in a largely uncontested example of global change?

Organizational Levels and Ethical Response

To date, most specifically Christian response to global environmental change has been in the realms of Christian ethics, Christian attempts to influence national policies, Christian education, and in development-oriented foreign missions. Yet, do we know, in this unfortunate, slowly emptying vast kettle of fish, *what ethical values and concepts of virtue and duty are already operational or widely accepted?*

Before we begin marching up and down on the dock and shouting "The earth is the Lord's, repent of your nets!" Christians should, as part of the practice of econormative ethics, investigate the way community ethical norms are structured and enforced in the fishing trade. Our interviews indicate, for example, that fishers have a well-developed concept of duties to others. Among themselves, the fishers value a strong work ethic, with its associated virtues such as hard work, determination, and dependability. Fishers value respect for the sea, including understanding how dangerous and unpredictable the ocean is, caring for fish stocks, and knowing "the ground." Engaging in a dangerous trade in a capricious environment, they appreciate safety, and exercise caution by avoiding unnecessary risks and maintaining their vessels well.

Among their secondary virtues are frugality, such as releasing undersized fish unharmed, avoiding wasteful by-catch, and caring for non-target species (except competitors and species that interfere with fishing). In Ireland, fishers are strongly protective of sea birds, and in the Pacific Northwest, fishers are protective of charismatic megafauna such as whales, ocean sunfish, and sea turtles. Many fishers encourage sharing both bounty and consolation in sorrow among the community. Experienced skippers consider it an obligation to aid individuals and vessels in distress. In addition, fishers report they "love" the ocean, or they find it beautiful or interesting. Are these the greedy, exploitation driven, self-actualizers of the "tragedy of the commons"? From a Christian perspective, the fishers do not need to be convinced that either the fish or the ocean have value or worth. They have a special bond with their tempestuous, unforgiving beloved. The ocean is "in their blood." So what, if anything, is dysfunctional in this scenario?

First, as fisheries decline progresses, the fishers' communitarian ethos of respect for one's crew is largely replaced by material values, such as owning a large vessel. Traditional fishers have little concept of a "bad" fisher, but in stressed fisheries, accusations of wrongdoing include greed and not answering distress calls. In Ireland, as the fisheries collapse, job satisfaction, ties to Christianity, positive views of fishers, and beliefs that the local community supports the fishing trade all radically decline.

Second, despite the camaraderie on individual boats, communication between stakeholders and regions is fraught with contention and discord. The Irish, for example, are in competition with other members of the European Union for quotas and catches. They consider themselves ill-equipped, in their small, family-owned boats, to face factory ships. Their circumstance is representative of many folk- or family-owned fishing operations, who find their catches depleted by the larger, deep-water international fleets. Folk fishers frequently suffer from economic development in other sectors, such as factories or municipalities that dump pollution in shallow bays, or tourist facilities that pour silt on reefs.

The vast majority of the U.S. fishers interviewed felt betrayed by their own state and federal governments, by the scientific community, and by "environmentalists." Although all the interested parties value the fish and the marine environment, the long sequence of management failures has led to tension-filled, intergroup competition, and a lack of constructive response at higher levels of social organization.

Internationally, folk fishers and the residents of poorer or "underdeveloped" coastal communities are among the most vulnerable to the negative impacts of globalization of the fishing industry. If the Irish and PNW fishers have trouble protecting or restoring their stocks, imagine the challenges for a fisher living at the edge of an Asian megacity, or operating a sail-driven craft off the African coast. The burgeoning populations of less industrially developed regions can encourage new entrants into folk fisheries, which may already be fully exploited. Development organizations, seeking new employment for food sources for the world's poor, are finding that many fisheries cannot absorb new entrants. At a time when the world's hungry and growing populations need more protein, humanity is rapidly stressing the oceans into an unproductive state.

Constructive Christian Response to Fisheries Crises

Assuming the church has many needs to serve, where could Christianity provide constructive assistance in fisheries ecology? At the dawn of the twenty-first century, Christians have two routes. One is to enter Christian dialog over global ecological concerns in order to stimulate a thoughtful and charitable response in the secular spheres of work, economy, and politics. The primary goal is to make Christians better citizens (which will make Christian activism less obvious). The second is to attempt a distinctively Christian reply, utilizing Christian institutions or fellowships as an organizational base. Thus far Christians have

118

had limited success with the latter strategy, when they have attempted to create Christian environmental advocacy organizations as a replacement for the nonreligious variety. Efforts at environmental education staged by Christian educational consortia, such as AuSable Institute, have, in contrast, become well established and have sent well-informed students back to their home congregations.

If a distinctively Christian approach is implemented, taking a global issue from the top could be overwhelming. Therefore, Christians need to carefully select the level of social organization and the specific needs they intend to serve. Christian institutions (as opposed to Christians working professionally in the various maritime fields) are unlikely to make major contributions to the already massive literature on fish ecology, ocean pollution, or The Law of the Sea. Christian educational institutions, parachurch organizations, and denominations could, however, help fill five major needs: inter-community peacekeeping and conflict resolution, community healing and team building, ecosystem restoration, advocacy for poor and folk fishers who have little voice in fisheries politics dominated by long-distance fleets, and education of folk and family fishers to assist them in protecting their livelihood, as well as the food resources on which they and their neighbors depend.

One of the most serious barriers to fisheries restoration, for example, is intergroup antagonisms among stakeholders in the marine industries. Commercial fishers believe environmentalists to be disinterested in the economic needs of working seafarers, so the two factions rarely unite to sponsor restoration projects or to battle pollution. Fishers may be suspicious of NGOs because of past experiences with environmental lobbying for reduced quotas or more limited seasons.

The greatest ethical needs in global fisheries include peacekeeping, releasing anger, forgiving the sins of others, and renewal of relationships. Christians trained in conflict resolution and consensus construction could assist by developing forums for intergroup encounter and reconciliation. Churches working together could pursue community healing among fishers, and help to create dialogs between stakeholders that resolve old grudges, while acknowledging the human and environmental impacts of past conflicts and management failures. Christians might serve as "disinterested" facilitators to improve communication between the scientific establishment, the governments, and the fishers.

The maritime anthropology and policy literature indicates that intra- and inter-community dialog and team building can be effective in reducing overharvest and environmental degradation. Among our U.S. interviewees, regulations and cooperation among fishers has reduced competition between charter boats (the recreational sector) and trawlers. When the charter fishers' association begins to interact in a friendly way with the draggers' (bottom trawlers) association, care of the stocks begins to improve.

Similarly, the policy literature reports efforts by New England lobster fishers to develop a sustainable fishery. One of their methods is a division of space and catches into "lobster fiefs" among the interested fishers, who then prevent overharvest in their own territory. Should a fisher violate the fishing territory of someone else, the lobstermen use "moral suasion" to bring the pirate into line. Folk management is not always the best model for formal exogenous regulation of a fishery, but intergroup cooperation among stakeholders is the only way to restore a degraded ecosystem and keep it healthy once it recovers.

Christians could also organize cross-cultural contacts and community building events and organizations, in some cases, incorporating leadership from other religions. Many First Nations fishers are Christians, and most Native Americans, Christians and non-Christians, honor their own tribal religions and beliefs. In the Pacific Northwest, interreligious teams could develop peacekeeping activities that are fully respectful of the diverse backgrounds of the fishers. The Catholic diocese of Boston, for example, has attempted to help lobstermen organize to protect both lobster stocks and their continued participation in the trade. One wonders if a coordinated ministry to ease social turmoil among fishers would help to improve intergroup stresses. The fishers and the fish could benefit from a multilingual chaplain, and some shared rituals. A recent volume discussing collaborative community projects termed such strategies "the ecology of hope" (Bernard and Young, 1997). Encouraging Christian congregations to participate in environmental restoration activities builds healthy communities and socially conscious Christian youth.

Implications for Christian Institutions

The fishing case brings up the prickly question of whether Christian institutions themselves are in need of restructuring in the face of globalization. In the U.S., Christian organizations have served as advocates for miners, have helped to politically focus family farmers in times of economic stress, and have provided a voice for inner-city residents smothered by lead or carbon monoxide. Christians have been leaders of the ecojustice movement, primarily because a number of denominations and parachurch organizations have made long-term commitments to assisting the socially marginalized — including farm workers, recent immigrants, and the urban and rural poor.

The greatest Christian environmental successes to date have originated in grass-roots responses to obvious degradations of both the natural world and human quality of life. The World Council of Churches has responded to many of the issues, as have individual denominations. In the fisheries case, however, Christian institutions have little expertise. Environmental ethicists and policy experts are already discussing concepts such as "environmental ethics in the global marketplace" (Dallmeyer and Ike, 1998), "managing the global commons" (Baden and Noonan, 1998), and "the internationalization of environmental protection" (Schreurs and Economy, 1997). One possibility is for Christians to raise their level of social organization by gathering regional or international working groups to develop and test strategies for ministry. An example might be a seminary-sponsored, inter-institutional project on encouraging cooperation between Christian fellowships in improving cooperation among fisheries stakeholders.

Our seminary and Christian college students can access the massive literature on fisheries policy and development anytime. Yet, they lack experience with fishers, watershed projects, and even the day-to-day workings of the fisheries extension and development establishment, such as FAO, the National Marine Fisheries Service, and state fisheries departments, who are attempting to deal with the conflict-ridden trade. We should consider adding more field training to expose students, particularly seminary enrollees, to the human devastation radical ecological change can cause in an entire region. Christian ethical education could increasingly incorporate a case-based approach that includes attempts to alter the social and economic sources of community disintegration, and of ecosystem degradation. Students who have visited sewage outfalls, and have talked to representatives of corporations, First Nations, and family fishers are more likely to engage in real community building than those who haven't. Students who have seen sea turtles drown as by-catch, watched salmon trying to climb fish ladders on dams, or have spoken with fishers devastated by the loss of their mortgages on their vessels will be less cavalier about how well buffered the environment is in the face of new technologies. To raise a generation of environmental peacekeepers requires rethinking the way we teach social ethics, and splicing together components of Christian education now separated among the departments of ethics and theology, church and society, Christian counseling and international missions.

Offering constructive assistance internationally is one of the greatest challenges to Christianity at the dawn of its third millennium. Christian missions have already helped to establish many aquaculture programs, and have assisted family fishers in establishing cooperatives to improve their sales prices, and have encouraged innovations in capture and storage technologies. Christian NGOs are thus already oriented toward FAO goals, such as organizing artisanal fishers, improving the quality of fish as food, spreading aquaculture, and protecting key spawning sites (Le Sann, 1998). Development advisors will see their work undone, however, if the water quality of near-shore waters in the "South" continues to deteriorate, and international fleets continue to plow the southern seas.

Two areas where Christian international effort might be expanded are, again, in the cooperative nature of fisheries management and in education. This could include acting as facilitators to improve stakeholder communication in regions, such as the west coast of Africa, where many forms of marine harvest are declining. Advocacy for poorer, artisanal or folk fishers can only help those who already have a very limited share of the catch. Environmental change has long been a root cause of social injustice, and the fisheries case exemplifies the continuing potential negative impact of international businesses on the resources available to the poor. Again, working groups identified with fisheries management are superior to scattered individuals in a mix of organizational settings in wrestling with the tangled politics.

With the arrival of the Internet, for good or for ill, Christians could restructure the form of their educational outreach, particularly in less industrialized nations. Establishing high school and junior college level technical training programs for fishers could help to slow environmental abuses, and could also make the fishers themselves aware of the science of marine biology and ecosystem management, the impacts of the global markets, and their need to organize. Conveyed to the fishers and adapted to regional contexts, this knowledge could prevent many disasters, and would make fishers more aware of the need for active environmental protection.

AuSable Institute, which offers environmental training to students from a consortium of Christian colleges, has set up a cooperative field education program with a college in India. More such international links are desperately needed, and would give greater environmental encouragement to Christians from non-Euroamerican backgrounds. One of the advantages of globalization is that an institution based in Seattle or Marakesh can convey training materials to any of the world's coasts.

The Biblical Heritage

I would like to conclude by invoking the Beatitudes of Matthew 5 and related texts such as Luke 6, "the blessings and woes," that encourage Christian responsibility towards and sacrifice for the good of the greater society. When Jesus said, "Blessed are the peacemakers, for they will be called the children of God" (Mt 5:9), he recognized that peacemakers would have no easy task, and that to receive God's inheritance as "sons" they would risk all they had. This passage also recognizes that there are spiritual callings which transcend politics. When Jesus said, "Blessed are you who hunger now, for you will be satisfied . . ." (Lk 6), he was speaking to an audience where hunger was far more than spiritual; he was addressing common folks whose fish had been taken by others, and whose nets often came up empty. Rather than denying global change or wishing it away as too massive to control, Christians should see the process as both a challenge and a new call to ministry.

Works Cited

Baden, J. A., and D. S. Noonan. *Managing the Commons*. Bloomington: University of Indiana Press, 1998.

Bernard, T., and J. Young. *The Ecology of Hope: Communities Collaborate for Sustainability*. East Haven, CT: New Society Publishers, 1997.

Bratton, S. P. *Six Billion and More: Human Population Regulation and Christian Ethics*. Louisville: Westminster/John Knox, 1992.

Dallmeyer, D. G., and A. F. Ike. *Environmental Ethics and the Global Marketplace*. Athens, GA: The University of Georgia Press, 1998.

Derr, T., and J. Nash. *Environmental Ethics and Christian Humanism*. Nashville: Abingdon Press, 1996.

Le Sann, A. *A Livelihood from Fishing: Globalization and Sustainable Fisheries Policies*. London: Intermediate Technology Publications, 1998.

Schreurs, M. A., and E. C. Economy. *The Internationalization of Environmental Protection*. Cambridge Studies in International Relations, no. 52. Cambridge: Cambridge University Press, 1997.

Additional Resources

Berrill, M. *The Plundered Seas: Can the World's Fish be Saved?* San Francisco: Sierra Club Books, 1997.

Engel, J. R., and J. G. Engel. *Ethics of Environment and Development*. Tucson: University of Arizona Press, 1990.

Hallman, D. *Ecotheology: Voices from South and North*. Maryknoll, NY: Orbis Press, 1994.

Hampson, F. O., and J. Reppy. *Earthly Goods: Environmental Change and Social Justice*. Ithaca, NY: Cornell University Press, 1996.

McGoodwin, J. *Crisis in the World's Fisheries: People, Problems and Policies*. Syracuse, NY: Syracuse University Press, 1990.

Rasmussen, L. L. *Earth Community/Earth Ethics*. Maryknoll, NY: Orbis Books, 1996.

9

The Spirit, Globalization, and the Future of Medicine

ALLEN VERHEY

"If we live by the Spirit, let us also be guided by the Spirit" (Gal 5:25). So Paul advised some Christians in Galatia in the middle of the first century. It's still good advice. Let it be the text — or at least the pretext — for these remarks as I make some suggestions about where the Spirit may be leading the church in response to the expanding powers of medicine in a shrinking world.

We Live by the Spirit

We must begin by acknowledging the reality and power of death in the world, for it is against the power of death that the church affirms that "we live by the Spirit." However many changes have taken place between the first century and the twenty-first, whatever differences mark human beings and cultures around the world, they are alike in this: people die. Death and its forerunners, sickness and suffering, threaten to alienate us from our own flesh, from our communities, and from God. If death is our destiny, then so is alienation. To its great credit, medicine resists death — but if there is no other and better sense of destiny, then the resistance medicine offers is undertaken under the power of death, under the tyranny of survival, with the desperation of hopelessness. And then medicine becomes — ironically — a place where death makes its power felt by alienating patients from their bodies, from their communities, and from their God — before the end of their lives and for the sake of their survival.

The last word, it seems, belongs to death, and the horror of it is not simply the termination of existence, but the unraveling of meaning, the destruction of relationships, the lordship of chaos. It is the light that seems ephemeral; it is the darkness that seems to surround and overcome the light and the life. Then we are right to be fearful of death, and to tremble before its messengers.

Christians claim, however, that it is not so, that the last word is not death. They believe, as they say in the Nicene Creed, "in the Holy Spirit, the Lord and Giver of life," and in the Apostles' Creed they list among the works of the Spirit "the resurrection of the body and the life everlasting." Christians have — and their creeds have — quite a different sense of an ending; they affirm that "we live by the Spirit." Christians do not deny the reality of death — or the ways it threatens human beings in their relationships with their own bodies and with their communities and with God. Nevertheless, Christians make the audacious (and finally hilarious) claim that the last word belongs to God and to the life-giving and gracious Spirit of God. The last word, then, is not death but life, not alienation and suffering but *shalom*.

In the context of God's gift of shalom, one aspect of the Spirit's work in creating the church is this: the church was — and is called to be — a community of healing. In memory of Jesus and in the power of the Spirit it could hardly be otherwise. In memory and in hope the church continued the healing ministry of Jesus, and healing continued to be a sign of God's good future. The church remembered Jesus' instruction for mission: "heal the sick . . . and say to them, 'The Kingdom of God has come near to you'" (Lk 10:9; cf. Mt 10:7-8). Hard on the heels of Pentecost there is healing (Acts 3:1-10). And the promise of the Spirit was always the promise of Christ, that the whole creation will be made new, that death shall be no more, that neither mourning nor crying nor pain shall be anymore (Rev 21:4), and that "our bodies" will be redeemed (Rom 8:23). The church entered the world as a religion of healing. Healing was — and is — as much the vocation of Christian community as preaching. And when in the power of the Spirit people were healed, there was a foretaste of God's good future.

126

Of course, it was not yet that good future. The power of death continued to assert its doomed reign. The continuing power of death evidently prompted a crisis of hope in the Thessalonian church. People still die, the Thessalonians observed. Paul's reply reminded them that the basis for hope is not some power we have at our disposal but "that Jesus died and rose again" (1 Thess 4:9), and he assured them that even the dead have not been abandoned, that even death cannot separate them from the love and power of God (cf. Rom 8:38). While death asserts its doomed reign, the church must wait and watch for God's good future, for that harvest of which the resurrection of Jesus and the gift of the Spirit are "first fruits." To "wait" is not to do nothing. To wait is to delight in what healings there are as tokens of God's future without supposing that the power to heal is simply at our disposal. To wait is to comfort the grieving (1 Thess 4:18) and to "help the weak" (1 Thess 5:14). To wait under the sign of the cross is to share the suffering of those who hurt; to wait is compassion.

The Spirit *is* there in the promise that the whole creation will be made new, that death shall be no more (Rev 21:4), and that "our bodies" will be redeemed (Rom 8:23). The Spirit *is* there wherever the fulfillment of that promise is given token — where the sick are healed, where the grieving are comforted, where the threat of death is met with confidence in God and with care for persons as embodied and communal selves.

Remembering the Mission of the Church

When the church went out into the world as a community of healing, it discovered a variety of healing practices. Its mission required that it think about and talk about these alternative practices. The church accepted miracle, of course, but it claimed that all healing comes from the God of creation and covenant, the God of Jesus and the Spirit. It was not by the power of Asclepius or Serapis that people were healed but by the power of God. The early church rejected magical healing practices even when it was the name of Jesus that was invoked in a magical incantation. And it accommodated medicine without surrendering its conviction that all healing comes from God. Most Christians followed the sage advice of Jesus ben Sirach, who regarded physicians and their medicines as instruments of God (Ecclesiasticus 38:1-14).

The church's acceptance of medicine as a form of healing did not mean, of course, that anything and everything "medical" was approved. When the church called Jesus "the Great Physician," it honored physicians, especially the "Hippocratic" physicians, commending their compassion and their commitment to the patient's good, but it also provided a model for medicine that set it in the context of a story that reached from creation to resurrection and God's good future.

Within that story the body and its health were regarded as great goods, but as part of a larger good, not as the *summum bonum*. And sickness was not regarded as the greatest evil, but as a feature of the disorder introduced by human sin, as part of a larger evil. Although physical affliction is an evil, it might, by the grace of God, remind people of their finitude, their dependence, and indeed, of their sinfulness, of the disorder that infects the relations of persons to their bodies, to each other, and to God.

Christians did not consider the practices of physicians *de novo*. Among contending accounts of the appropriate conduct of physicians the church adopted and adapted the medical ethic epitomized by the Hippocratic Oath. The ascendancy of the Oath itself in the Western tradition of medicine is probably a result of the rise of Christianity. The church supported this tradition — but also modified it. One such modification was described by Henry Sigerist as "the most revolutionary and decisive change" in Western medicine, namely, that the sick were ascribed "a preferential position" (Sigerist, 1943, pp. 69-70).

Jesus was, after all, not just a healer, not just "the Great Physician"; he was also one who suffered and died. Remembering Jesus' suffering and death, Christians saw in the sick the very image of their Lord and discerned in their care for them (or in their abandoning them) an image of their care for Christ himself (or for their abandoning Christ himself). The classic passage, of course, is Matthew 25:31-45. The passage was explicitly cited, for example, in *The Rule of St. Benedict* to care for the sick "as if it were Christ himself who was served" (ch. 36). And the passage was surely reflected in the conduct of Christians during the outbreak of plague in the third century, "visiting the sick without a thought as to the danger," as the bishop of Alexandria reported. To be guided by the Spirit in memory of Jesus has always led Christian community along the path of care for the sick.

Because care for the sick was a duty, the church required competence and diligence of physicians. The medieval penitential literature, for example, required physicians to confess incompetence and negligence. Care for the sick required good medical care, but it could not be reduced to medical care. And although health and life were great goods, they were not the greatest goods, and neither physicians nor patients were permitted to seek them in ways that violated some greater or larger good.

Jesus was not only a healer, not only one who suffered, but also a preacher of good news to the poor" (Lk 4:18); and his words of blessing to the poor were no less a token and a promise of God's good future than his works of healing (e.g., Lk 6:20). The poor along with the sick were accorded a "preferential position" in memory of Jesus, and fidelity to God required that the needs of the sick poor not be forgotten, neither by physicians nor by their communities.

So clergy frequently took the lead in providing medical care for the sick and poor. The tradition of physician clergy stretched from the early Middle Ages into the modern period, and it was largely devoted to the care of the sick poor. The hospital itself has its origin in the Christian concern for the poor. In the fourth century, Christian communities began to establish *xenodocheia* (or hospices) to feed and shelter the poor. In 372 Basil the Great founded a vast *xenodocheia*, the Basileias, with buildings to care for the sick poor (and separate buildings for contagious and non-contagious diseases), and with a staff that included physicians. It was the prototype of many other such Christian and civil institutions.

In the development of a medical mission within the missionary movement of the nineteenth century the church retrieved its vocation as a community of healing. The first medical missionaries were evidently sent to care for the "real" missionary and his family, but before long the memory of Jesus' suffering and healing was retrieved and prompted a richer vision of the medical mission of the churches. As one medical missionary stated in 1888, "As [Christ's] ministry was a ministry of sympathy with suffering humanity, as He healed the sick, and went about continually doing good, . . . so His ambassadors must 'preach the Gospel,' not by word alone, but likewise, by a compassionate

129

Christ-like ministry, performed in Christ's name and for His sake" (Lowe, 1888, p. 104).

The medical mission in the nineteenth century frequently involved a clinic in an isolated context. Only curative medicine was practiced because there was not enough time for — and little understanding of — anything else. In the twentieth century, with the expanding powers of medicine, the clinics grew into hospitals and into an educational mission to help train native physicians and nurses. The isolation has all but disappeared, as mass communication shrank the world. Medical missionaries, of course, even when isolated, encountered other communities and traditions of healing; they rejected magic, sometimes found themselves in competition with local traditions of healing, and sometimes found ways to accommodate local traditions and to cooperate with them. As the globalization of communication made the world smaller, it also spread Western medicine and the expectations that it prompts; in that context medical missionaries often competed with civic health programs but eventually discovered ways to cooperate with them. It should also be observed that curative medicine has been supplemented with programs in rehabilitation and prevention, including sanitation, nutrition, and vaccination. There is much in the history of medical missions to celebrate — and much in the tradition of medical missions to hold on to as the centuries turn again and as medical powers continue to expand in a world that continues to shrink.

There is also, however, much to rue, much to repent as the centuries turn again. The missionary movement was frequently infected with the imperialistic attitudes of the nineteenth century. It sometimes created a global community of patrons and clients, rather than a global community of friends. It sometimes yielded to the temptation of the "conceit of philanthropy," dividing the world into needy and benighted beneficiaries and powerful and enlightened benefactors. It sometimes, therefore, was readier to speak than to listen, readier to teach than to learn. Medical missions were sometimes undertaken with triumphalist assumptions about the progress of European civilization. They sometimes identified and confused Western medicine with the good future of God. They sometimes transplanted inappropriate technologies and focused on rescue medicine rather than on the causes of sickness. But for all of these faults, one may discern in medical missions the memory and hope that the Spirit gives, a mission of the church as a global community of peaceable difference, as a community of moral discourse, and as a community of healing.

In the last half of the twentieth century, when hospitals became showcases for medical technology and patient care became increasingly "medicalized," theologians retrieved important elements of the tradition of the Christian community's encounter with medicine. Against the reduction of patients to their pathologies, they retrieved the professional commitment of fidelity to patients as *persons* (and underscored consent as a fundamental component of fidelity). And against the subsequent reduction of persons to their capacities for agency, they insisted on embodiment. The churches and their theologians have consistently reiterated the tradition's concern for the poor in debates about access to health care. Developments in technology continue to raise dramatic questions for the church and her theologians, but as the church goes into the next century, it will be important to recognize a shrinking world as well as the expanding powers of medicine. It will be important for the church to be faithful to its mission, to be a global community of peaceable difference, to be a community of moral discourse, and to be a community of healing.

Church, Medicine, and Globalization Tomorrow

As a community of healing in a global context, the church will continue to encounter other traditions and communities of healing. If globalization includes not just the phenomenon of a shrinking world but also "modernization," or the spread of technical rationality, then Western medicine will have a certain priority among the traditions and communities of healing. In this context the church must continue to affirm that all healing comes from God. It may and must, therefore, celebrate the contributions of Western medicine to health, and it may and must continue in its medical missions to cooperate in medical training programs. However, it must not allow itself as a community of healing simply to be identified with Western medicine; it must be ready also to be critical of Western medicine.

In the first place, the readiness to be critical of the tradition of medicine with which medical missions have largely been associated is important to the conversation with other communities and traditions of healing. Unless a capacity for self-critical reflection is preserved, the expectation of an honest and fruitful dialogue with others is diminished. Those who would teach have much to learn.

There is a second reason that the church as a community of healing must not allow itself simply to be identified with Western medicine. Because health is not primarily "medical," the mission of the church as a healing community in a global context may not be purely or even primarily "medical." The primary causes of illness in the world are poverty, violence, pollution, and behavior. Many of the improvements in health in the United States during the nineteenth and twentieth centuries, for example, can be attributed to rising living standards, better nutrition, sanitation, and falling birth rates. A community of health in a global context has an agenda that cannot be purely or even primarily "medical." The mission of the church must include cooperation in sustainable economic development, agricultural development, nutritional programs, sanitation programs, and peacemaking.

Here, too, however, it will be important for the church to preserve the capacity for self-critical reflection about the Western and triumphalist assumptions sometimes carried by the metaphor of "development." "Development" is an image taken from the maturation of an organism, and it may suggest that the most modern nations, like the United States, are the most "mature," the most civilized, and therefore models to imitate. Moreover, "development" has sometimes functioned as a powerful secular religion, as "the focus of redemptive hopes and expectations," to use the words of Peter Berger in *Pyramids of Sacrifice* (1976, p. 17).

Development as a secular religion assumes that human fulfillment is to be found in activities that improve material living conditions. The church as a community of health may not neglect the material living conditions important to health, but it must and may nurture conversations that define the goals of development in qualitative terms as well as quantitative goods. It must remember in its own discourse and remind others that the "good life" may not be reduced to material goods or even to "health" as the *summum bonum*, that it includes goods such as truth, beauty, friendship, humility, and simplicity. Again, of course, those who would teach have much to learn.

There is, moreover, a third reason that the church must not simply identify with Western medicine. Western medicine is, as we have seen, sometimes co-opted by the very power of death that it resists. Because that is so, the church as a healing community must articulate a different and a better destiny as a context for the worthy practice of medicine. The church needs to preserve a prophetic distance from Western medicine even as it utilizes it in priestly service. Western medicine has sat at the feet of Francis Bacon, and it has learned to regard knowledge as power over nature and to assume that such knowledge (or technology) leads inevitably toward human well-being. In such an account of the world the fault that runs through our life and through our globe lies in nature, and our hope lies in technology. That is a creed ripe for doubt.

Compassion is a visceral response to the suffering of another; it moves us to do *something*, but it does not tell us *what* thing to do. For centuries human beings were almost helpless in the face of disease and death. Some were simply "overmastered by their diseases," to quote an ancient Hippocratic treatise. Then Francis Bacon made an innovative suggestion. He urged the rejection of that old category of one "overmastered" by disease, and he insisted that to call any disease "incurable" "licenses neglect and inattention and exempts ignorance from discredit." Compassion prompted the gradual development of a medical science and technology that no longer leave us quite so helpless and hopeless in the face of the sad stories of human suffering and premature dying.

The most obvious failure of a compassion trained by Bacon, with its pervasive expectation that suffering can be avoided or ended, is the simple truth that technology does not provide an escape either from our mortality or altogether from our suffering. Not every sad story of human suffering and premature dying has a happy ending with the help of medical technology, after all; some of us, and finally all of us, are "overmastered by our diseases," in spite of Bacon. This is obvious, I say, but we have not been disposed to acknowledge the obvious. Our enthusiasm for technology as a response to suffering has blinded us to the limits of technology.

Given our confidence in technology and our expectations, compassion moves those unskilled in medical technology to assign the sufferer to the care of medicine, to those armed with artifice. So, the community abandons the sufferer to medicine — and removes the suffering one. This

133

modern compassion then moves those skilled with such tools, those armed with artifice, to attempt to give the story a happy ending by their technology. And if and when they fail, it licenses their withdrawal, since they cannot do the patient any "good" any more — as if the only "good" were the elimination of mortality and suffering. Meanwhile, such patients, abandoned by both friends and experts, and surrounded by technology rather than by a community that knows and shares their suffering, suffer alone and pointlessly. It is not surprising, perhaps, that modern "compassion" looks for a technological solution to end that suffering, too — a final solution, the elimination of suffering by eliminating the sufferer.

Both Western medicine and the Western church need to relearn an ancient virtue and to equip compassion not only with artifice but also with some ancient wisdom about life in a mortal body and in community. There is much to relearn concerning compassion in the memory of Jesus that the Spirit gives, and much to learn from communities across the globe. The church has made too little place for lament in its liturgy; it has too often pretended to possess a perfection that denies the "not yet" character of our medicine and of our lives. The result has sometimes been the alienation of those who suffer and have difficulty lifting themselves by their bootstraps to the heights of some triumphant liturgy. Those who would teach have much to learn. Even so, the church has an account of human destiny that acknowledges the power of the life-giving Spirit of God and can provide a context for both compassion and its use of tools, lest, in medicine's resistance to death it prematurely alienates people from their own bodies and from their communities.

The church as a community of healing has an agenda that is not purely or even mainly medical. Even so, because medicine does make a real, if small, contribution to health, the church continues to have a mission, a vocation, that is partly medical. The prophetic voice of the church will protest the idolatry of technology, but it will not regard technology as demonic. When compassion is equipped with wisdom and with piety, it will not reject all artifice.

The church has frequently told the story of the Good Samaritan as a model for health care and has struggled to live it in its medical mission. It's a good story. On the other hand, in the context of expanding medical powers and limited resources it seems an odd story. Compassion can lead to costly care. We understand this well enough, perhaps even better than the Samaritan did, for we have today an assortment of technologies to help and to heal which make donkeys, oil and wine, and the binding of wounds seem simply quaint. Moreover, to these technologies are attached costs that make the Samaritan's two denarii seem laughable (even if it was two days' wages for an agricultural worker). Can the church live the story it loves to tell in a global context? Or are there simply too many along the side of the road? Can we still be Good Samaritans, or even just Fair Samaritans, in the midst of tragic choices imposed by the scarcity of resources and the greatness of need in the global village?

The answer, I think, is that we can still be Good Samaritans — but not without attention to policy. To be good, a Samaritan who encountered stranger after stranger left "half-dead" by the side of the road would have to give some attention to policy. The Samaritan's compassion would finally insist on some consideration of policy, perhaps increased police protection along the Jericho Road but also perhaps health care policies that would assure the needy access to an inn or at least not penalize a hospitable innkeeper. The very compassion that moved the Samaritan to care for the injured one would motivate attention to policy when *many* hurt. The global Good Samaritan will be attentive to policy.

Let me quickly mention two caveats. First, no particular policy is simply given with the story. The details of policy are not magically provided by compassion. Second, the story may not be reduced to policy. The story is lived not just in policy formation, but in the formation of health care ministries among the poor, in village clinics staffed by contemporary Good Samaritans. The story is lived not just where public programs are instituted but where doctors and nurses learn to see their work not only as a collection of skills but as a form of discipleship which attends to the needs of the sick poor.

No policy is simply given with the story. The story may not be reduced to policy. Still, those who tell the story and delight in it should not neglect it when they consider policy. The story not only motivates attention to policy; it also helps to form the church's attention to policy. It forms, first and most obviously, a prophetic protest against injustice. The church may and must help bolster public attention to health care access by speaking sometimes prophetically, raising their voice against injustices. The inequities of the shrinking world may not be forgotten.

That the West has been a net exporter of disease and an importer of resources may not be overlooked. There is a past that needs repenting of: the marketing of infant formula that changed behaviors about breast-feeding, the continuing commerce in tobacco, the exporting of waste for disposal, and the emigration of health professionals to the West. There is a future to be warned against, such as the commodification and commercialization of body parts.

The global Good Samaritan will need to nurture virtues besides compassion to be good, and to form good policy. The first of them is truthfulness, the readiness to acknowledge the truth about our world and our medicine, about the limits imposed by our mortality and by the finitude of our resources. The twin of truthfulness is humility, the readiness to acknowledge that we are not gods but creatures of God, finite and mortal creatures in need finally of God's care, and watching finally for God's future. Joined to both is gratitude, the thankfulness for the opportunities within our limits, opportunities to care for one conventionally regarded as among "the least of these." We have come around again to compassion, to care. The Samaritan will never be good without compassion, without love, for the neighbor.

Jesus was asked, "But who is my neighbor?" It is a question of great importance in a shrinking world. He replied with the story of the Good Samaritan and with a question of his own, "Who was a neighbor to the one left half-dead?" Notice two things here: First, the Samaritan *was* a neighbor, not just a stranger, not simply an enemy. The story is that we *are* neighbors to each other, even to those we no not know. The Spirit creates a global community of peaceable difference, a community of neighbors and friends. Second, the answer to the question "Who is my neighbor?" comes indirectly; it comes not so much by theoretical analysis as by a readiness to care for another as though they were a neighbor. The global Good Samaritan will discover neighbors and friends in a shrinking world by caring for them.

The global Good Samaritan will never be good without compassion, but let it be said again: The Samaritan will never be good with just compassion. That is, of course, precisely the wrong way to put it. The contemporary Samaritan will never be good with *only* compassion, but a *just* compassion is indeed required. The virtue of justice is essential to those who would be (even) Fair Samaritans.

To the discourse about policy the church brings convictions learned at Pentecost. In memory and hope it looks for the curse of Babel to be lifted. It does not, like the Enlightenment, assume that all must first agree about some universal and purely rational principles before we can come to understand each other. It does not, like the postmodernist, presume that there is no hope of communication across our differences. In the context of the asymmetries of power in the global village, the church may and must, in its own discourse and in its conversations with others, listen carefully to the voice of the stranger and especially to the voices and concerns of those who are least well off.

The story is lived not only where Christians speak sometimes prophetically, not only when they speak sometimes sagely, not only when they speak morally, but also when they speak sometimes politically, using policy analysis and compromise to preserve or to accomplish some little good for those who hurt and to avert some great harm toward which pride and envy still tilt the world. If we live by the Spirit, let us also be guided by it. To be guided by the Spirit still means to remember and to hope and, remembering and hoping, to struggle against the evils that threaten our embodied life and our common life in the global village.

Works Cited

Berger, Peter. *Pyramids of Sacrifice.* Garden City, NJ: Anchor Doubleday, 1976.

Lowe, John, in James Johnson, ed., *Report of the Centenary Conference on the Protestant Missions of the World* (London, 1888), vol. 2, cited in C. Peter Williams, "Healing and Evangelism: The Place of Medicine in Later Victorian Protestant Missionary Thinking," in W. J. Sheils, ed. *The Church and Healing.* Oxford: Basil Blackwell, 1982.

Sigerist, Henry. *Civilization and Disease.* Ithaca, NY: Cornell University Press, 1943.

For Further Reading

Marty, Martin, and Kenneth Vaux, eds. *Health/Medicine and the Faith Traditions.* Philadelphia, 1982.

May, William F. "The Sacral Power of Death in Contemporary Experience," in Stephen E. Lammers and Allen Verhey, eds. *On Moral Medicine,* 2nd ed. Grand Rapids: Eerdmans, 1998.

Mohrmann, Margaret. *Medicine as Ministry.* Cleveland: Pilgrim Press, 1995.

Temkin, O. *Hippocrates in a World of Pagans and Christians.* Baltimore: Johns Hopkins University Press, 1991.

IV

CHRIST, THE CHURCH,
AND OTHER RELIGIONS

Introduction

The encounter between the world's religions is not a new phenomenon. It is as old as humankind. Nor is discussion and theological reflection about the issues raised by this encounter something new. However, the collapse of the geographic divide between the world's religions — and especially the end of Western nations' religious isolation — is a twentieth-century development. The West is now as religiously pluralistic as the rest of the world. The interdependency of the global economy and the migration of people to locales promising better employment, better living conditions, and even more abundant supplies of water will serve to accentuate this intermingling of the world's religions during the coming decades. Every local church — whether in Kansas City or Kinshasa, in Toledo or Tokyo, in London or in Latvia — will serve in a religiously pluralist environment.

Several major faith traditions are now global religions — present in nearly every country, assuming distinctive forms in many different cultures. To serve in this era of globalization, every local church leader needs to be equipped for interreligious encounter. The beginning point for effective encounter is understanding. Without a basic comprehension of others' beliefs, our encounters will be characterized by prejudice, paternalism, and pride. Empathy, compassion, and honest dialogue are the fruit of understanding. As we begin to grasp the convictions of people whose faith is different than our own, we can't avoid being impressed by the earnestness and complexity of their pursuit of Truth.

Among the world's religions, in addition to Christianity, two stand out as global faiths — Buddhism and Islam. The articles in this section are written by three Christians who are respected throughout the world for their insight into faith traditions other than their own, and for the effectiveness of their interreligious dialogue. Though the authors do not attempt to offer all one needs for a foundational understanding of global religions, they provide fascinating insights that can guide local churches in their encounter with the adherents of global faiths who live next door.

Kosuke Koyama provides a basic summary of the beliefs of mainstream Buddhists. Central to interfaith encounter, he says, is the discussion of how we come to our religious convictions. How can human beings claim to know ultimate Truth? Koyama compares a Buddhist and a Christian understanding of revelation, contrasting the Enlightened One of Buddhism with the Anointed One of the Christian faith, and comparing the deep similarities and radical differences between the two approaches to religious knowledge. Equally central to interfaith encounter is the discussion of how one defines a "good" person and promotes virtuous moral behavior. Koyama outlines four ethical issues Buddhism and Christianity share in common, but to which they give significantly different answers. His discussion not only challenges Christian readers to address more fully the ethical implications of their own faith, but also to engage their Buddhist neighbors in dialogue with greater compassion and conviction.

Born a Muslim, and committing himself to the Christian faith as an adult, Lamin Sanneh understands from within both of these global faiths. Recognizing the centrality of Jesus for Christians, Sanneh opens for our understanding the place of Muhammad for Muslims, whose respect for their Prophet as the "bearer" of revelation and the "beautiful model" suggests that Christians at least appreciate what he means to Muslims. Sanneh suggests several strengths of Islam from which Christians could learn; he also portrays some of the unique contributions of Christianity as a global religion. Effective, honest, and harmonious encounter between Christians and Muslims is unquestionably one of the great needs of the coming decades. Sanneh's article provides some helpful guidance for this pursuit.

140

Turning from the encounter with other religions to encounter within our own, Mel Robeck traces essential steps along the path of improved ecumenical relations among Christian groups. After reviewing the recent history of ecumenism, he explores some new dynamics that will characterize the relationship between major Christian traditions. With the shift of global church leadership to the "two-thirds" world, new issues will dominate the ecumenical agenda. Robeck makes the hopeful prediction that the dominant desire will be for appropriate expressions of global Christian community.

Unquestionably, as globalization pushes us into more intense encounters with people radically different from ourselves, learning to understand and appreciate others is essential for human survival and well-being. The challenge to the church is whether we will intensify our balkanized, ethnically cleansed societies, or for once in history be known as the "blessed peacemakers."

Tim Dearborn

10

Observation and Revelation in Dialogue:
Towards a Christian Theological
Approach to Buddhism

KOSUKE KOYAMA

The Challenge for Christians to Understand
Global Religions and Global Ethics

The socioeconomic-political dimensions of globalization bring with them more intense encounters between global religions and ethics than ever before in history. Thus it is more imperative than ever that Christians develop an understanding of the ethical insights and foundations of other religions. Buddhism presents a fascinating case in point. For the "world religions," globalization is not a new experience. Buddhism, Christianity, and Islam are called universal religions. Here the word "universal" should be taken to indicate an ability to engage people in a universally persuasive discussion on human spiritual and moral life. This universality is not a geographical or statistical concept. Ethics and religion are intimately related. Both must inspire social *responsibility*. Religious messages must enable ethical engagement in specific social contexts.

An example of such Buddhist ethical engagement is seen in the work of Lily De Silva from Sri Lanka, who writes, "Maldistribution of

142

wealth is intrinsically evil because it destroys the rich through overconsumption and the poor through malnutrition" (De Silva, 1989, p. 41). Through this ethical concern, Buddhism participates in the globalization of ethics. On the Christian side, the words of Jesus, "Go and do likewise" (Lk 10:29-37) bid globalized ethical engagement.

What Is Buddhism?

Buddhism is the religion that is expressed through the cultured words that have accumulated around the person of the *Awakened One,* as Christianity is expressed through words about the *Anointed One.* There is as painful a gap, however, between the teaching of Buddhism and what Buddhists do as there is between Christian teaching and what Christians do. Neither Buddhists nor Christians can be said to necessarily live the life demonstrated by Buddha or Christ. The reality of Buddhism is to be found in the Buddhist with all that person's human shortcomings and brokenness. Buddhist Thailand, so defined by its national constitution, is today caught in a turmoil of bribery in politics and the AIDS epidemic, which could hardly be associated with Buddha, himself. Buddhism, the religion, is impervious to these calamities, but Buddhists are not. How seriously are the people of Thailand attentive today to the words of the Awakened One, which instruct that out of greed comes disorders in politics and health?

In order to appreciate Buddhism, it is necessary to grasp a simple outline of its central teachings. Scholars usually begin Buddhist study with the doctrine of *paticcasamuppada,* the Conditional Arising. The fundamental form of the doctrine is: "This being, that becomes; by the arising of this, that arises." "Ignorance" *(avijja),* "craving" *(tanha),* and "suffering" *(dukkha)* are the three prominent points of the Conditional Arising. This is the principle by which human existence is observed: namely, from ignorance comes craving and from craving comes suffering. This is the *diagnosis.* How, then, can this "mass of ill" be eliminated? Eliminate ignorance and craving will disappear. When craving disappears, suffering will disappear. This is the *therapy.* The tradition does not say from where ignorance comes. The ignorance of the Conditional Arising itself could be what ignorance means here.

The Four Noble Truths *(aryasatya)* are understood to be Buddha's reformulation of the truth of Conditional Arising for popular understanding. The doctrine of The Noble Truths begins with the truth of suffering *(dukkhasatya)*, and proceeds to the truth of the cause of suffering *(samudayasatya)*. After this diagnosis, it moves on to the therapy section. The third is the truth of the cessation of suffering *(nirodhasatya)*, and finally the truth of the path which leads to the cessation of suffering *(margasatya)*. Prominent in these formulations are three distinctive words linked to one another: ignorance, craving, and suffering.

The above description is central to Buddhist faith communities throughout the world. It is basically an *observation* on human life. In one of the most ancient texts we read, "If all attachment (by means of wisdom) is destroyed, (no further) suffering grows up" *(Udana, 1954)*. This, for the Buddhist, is the meaning of salvation. To know this is the awakening that will lead a person to *nirvana*, "a state of everlasting radiant smiles with nobody smiling" (the Thai monk, Buddhadasa Indapanno). Knowledge of the human predicament gained by this observation is the heart of the Buddhist tradition. Attachment is the undesirable "hot" condition of the soul. This is expressed in a remarkable piece of dialogue between the Buddha and his followers: "Monks, when one's turban or head is ablaze, what is to be done?" "Lord, when one's turban or head is ablaze, for the extinguishing thereof one must put forth extra desire, effort, endeavor, exertion, impulse, mindfulness, and attention" *(The Book of the Kindred Sayings, p. 372)*.

The ethical spirit of monastic Buddhism is to extinguish attachment. Monastic Buddhism moves towards this goal *(telos)* and, to that extent, is "hopeful." Buddhism accepts the Hindu doctrine of the *karman* (action and reaction). The *karman* works objectively. "If you do good, good will come to you; if you do evil, evil will come to you." The *karman* has positive and negative implications. If you extinguish the fire, good will come to you; if you do not, evil will come to you.

Mahayana Buddhism, appearing in northwest India about the second century CE, takes a different approach than monastic Buddhism, and intends to save all who are incapable of mustering the "extra desire, effort, endeavor . . . to extinguish the turban ablaze." In Mahayana Buddha the monk is transformed to Buddha, the savior of infinite mercy, who will gather all laypeople — those who are not *nirvana* specialists —

into the Great Vehicle *(mahayana)* to take them to the zone of "Wisdom Beyond" *prajnaparamita*.

The words "with extra desire, effort, endeavor . . ." suggest the presence of a moral self. This morally integral self is, however, only a constantly changing *aggregate (skandha)* of five elements: body, feeling, recognition, imagination, and discrimination. The self is impermanent *(anicca)* and in a constant state of change. There is a moral self, but not a substantive self *(anatta)*. This anthropology of no-self is expressed as *emptiness (sunyata)* in the Mahayana tradition. According to the great Mahayana philosopher Nagarjuna, *emptiness* is not the opposite of *fullness*. It "transcends and embraces both emptiness and fullness. . . . True Emptiness is wondrous Being" (Abe, 1985, p. 126). The source of human *freedom* is located in this wondrous emptiness.

Mahayana thought is not unrelated to the original monastic tradition. "When objects make contact with the eye, observe and identify them, and know what action has to be taken with whatever is seen. But don't permit like or dislike to arise. If you permit the arising of like, you will desire; if you permit the arising of dislike, you will want to destroy. Thus it is that there are likers and haters. This is what is called 'the self.' To go the way of the self is suffering and deception" (Indapanno, 1966, p. 7).

Either through the monastic development of insight or the Mahayana development of *emptiness* one may extinguish the fire of craving. The Buddhist *dharma* is observation of human life. Buddhism observes, gives diagnosis, and prescribes a therapy for human ills. It is not revelation-based religion, for religion "is a system of observation and practice" (Indapanno, 1967).

Comparison with the Christian Theological Approach

In the fascinating and complex encounter between Buddhism and Christianity, there are especially four areas where dialogue over ethics will be fruitful in our globalized future.

1. Observation and Revelation

One must not immediately insist that Buddhist *observation* and Christian *revelation* are in opposition to one another. In Christian theology, inspired by Christ's Two Natures, the relationship between the two is one of complementarity (dialogue) rather than opposition (monologue). Divine revelation cannot make itself meaningful apart from *human* observation. "Is there anyone among you who, if your child asks for a fish, will give a snake instead of a fish? [observation] . . . How much more will the heavenly Father give the Holy Spirit to those who ask him! [revelation]" (Lk 11:11-13). Calvin's *Institutes* and the Documents of Vatican II would not be possible apart from the observation of human life. Through the words of human observation the meaning of revelation is transmitted. The Sower in Jesus' parable would find the Buddhist warning (observation) of "the cares of the world and the lure of wealth" relevant (Mt 13:22).

On the other hand, one must recognize the discontinuity between observation and revelation uncompromisingly expressed in Matthew 16:17: "Blessed are you, Simon son of Jonah! For flesh and blood has not revealed this to you, but my Father in heaven." Christian theology thus recognizes two types of relationship between *observation* and *revelation:* Observation makes revelation meaningful, but revelation is beyond the reach of observation.

There is emotional and cultural difference in the perception of "discontinuity" between biblical and Buddhist teachings. Gandhi declared that he would not hesitate to reject even the authority of revealed scriptures "if it is repugnant to reason or moral sense" (Duncan, p. 178). There is a healthy connection between honest observation and rightly understood revelation. But how does one *rightly understand* revelation? Who can fathom the mind of God? asks St. Paul (Rom 11:34). To rightly observe human life is easier than to achieve a right understanding of revelation.

Because of a persistent human propensity for self-righteousness, revelation is too often subjected to fanaticism, inflicting serious damage to the spiritual and physical welfare of the human community. Though both observation and revelation can be captured by ideological fanaticism, the damage done by the misuse of revelation is greater since revelation contains the element of transcendence. It cannot be argued with. The Buddhist observation of human life has a quality that can check a fundamentalist monopolization of truth. The value of both observation and revelation is found in their power to create wholesomeness in human life. Ultimately, it is truth that creates wholesomeness in the human community. "The tree is known by its fruit" (Mt 12:34).

The statement that "according to Buddhism, human greed is destructive" is redundant because the truth that "human greed is destructive" can stand by itself. The universal *dharma* transcends the concern of "who said so." "The Buddha left no successors; his gift to posterity was the Dharma" (*Dialogue*, 1990). The historical Buddha is dispensable. The focus is on the *dharma*. Buddhism teaches "detachable truth." The *dharma* gains and retains its *dharma* quality by demonstrating universal validity in and by itself. *Ecce homo* (Jn 19:5) is unnecessary. Instead, *ecce dharma!* There is no profit in pursuing a "Quest for the Historical Gautama." The *dharma* once discovered can walk by itself as the scientific equation $E=mc^2$ is effective independently of Einstein.

"Greed brings prosperity," says the *falsa religione*. "Greed brings destruction," says the *vera religione*. Both Buddhism and Christianity are, in this sense, "true religions." "But God said to him, 'You fool! This very night your life is being demanded of you. And the things you have prepared, whose will they be?'" (Lk 12:20). Both intimate that to be authentically human is to battle against the power of greed. The *dharma* of the Conditional Arising warns of human greed. It proclaims this through the logic of cause and effect. The Buddhist observation belongs to the empiricist camp. Buddhism has no so-called "gap God" who tries to linger in the ever-diminishing space of mystery. "This being, that becomes" — is more central than the person of the Buddha.

The Christian concept of the truth is *attached* to the person of Jesus Christ. It expresses itself even in a quite unusual form: "Jesus Christ is the truth." For Christianity, the "Quest for the Historical Jesus" is inevitable. *Ecce homo* is essential. "Christianity" is a faith that confesses "Jesus is the Anointed One." Jesus is the truth-person who lived, was crucified, died, rose from the dead, and is exalted at the right hand of God. For Christians this life story is the truth. In contrast, confessing that "Gautama is the Awakened One," Buddhism invites us primarily to the *dharma*, not to the person of Gautama.

Is it important to know who said, "The Lord does not see as mortals see; they look on the outward appearance, but the Lord looks on the heart" (1 Sam 16:7)? Or "Let justice roll down like waters, and righteousness like an ever-flowing stream" (Amos 5:24)? Not necessarily. These verses can be meaningful irrespective of who uttered the words. Can "love you neighbor as yourself," or even "love your enemies" walk by itself as the Buddhist truth can? I contend that it can. These are inspiring words with universal validity, as much as the Buddhist critique of human greed. Even the parable of the Good Samaritan is powerful, whoever told it. It can stand without the name of Jesus Christ. This is a possibility.

Christian theology, however, *cannot* settle there. It has a scandalous element. In theology all words are engaged in history. They are not timeless, but timeful, as it were. In order to root our words in history, it is important to know who said this or that, and when/where. This is so because it is people that give reality to history. The mystery of history corresponds to that of the human person. Truth must be interpreted personally and historically. Christian theology is not interested in ahistorical impersonal truth. Can Christian teachings (doctrines), once formulated, become independent from history and fly around gravitation-free? No. They cannot. The ancient creeds insist upon this history-rooted character of the Christian truth by saying that Jesus *suffered under Pontius Pilate*. In his moment of death the martyr Stephen saw Jesus *standing* at the right hand of God (Acts 7:56). The urgency of history is symbolized by the risen Christ who is not sitting but standing.

2. Non-Theistic, No-Self Orientation

Often the contrast between the two faiths is expressed in terms of theistic Christianity and non-theistic Buddhism. "God" is present in Christianity, but absent in Buddhism. According to Buddhist teaching, as in Confucian teaching, "god-talk" is unprofitable and even a hindrance to the sincere pursuit of human fulfillment. "Fools say in their hearts, 'there is no God'" (Ps 14:1), we may say. But the Buddha and Confucius are not fools. The word "g-o-d" had different meanings for the Semitic and the Asian worlds.

The non-theistic, *not* atheistic, orientation of the Buddha (and Confucius) invites the question central to theological thinking: "What is God?" This question is generally expressed in Judeo-Christian thinking as "Which God is the true God?" and "Beloved, do not believe every spirit, but test the spirits to see whether they are from God" (1 Jn 4:1).

For Jews, Christians, and Muslims, God is *invisible*. The invisible God is beyond human comprehension. The Buddhist *dharma* is visible. The invisible God is mysterious and unpredictable, while the visible *dharma* is rational and predictable. The former suggests surprise and danger, the latter calmness and safety. The contrast is between an invisible *Person* ("Thus says the Lord . . .") and a visible *dharma* (diagnosis and therapy). With the invisible God, idolatry becomes a possibility because the human soul is tempted to manipulate such a God. The visible, knowable *dharma* does not incite idolatry. There is no passion or need to enhance or make visible that which is already visible. The human spirit does not live in an ambiguous relationship with the visible *dharma*.

When we ask the question, "What is God?" we risk "taking the name of God in vain" (Ex 20:7). "God is a Spirit, infinite, eternal, and unchangeable, in his being, wisdom, power, holiness, justice, goodness and truth" answers the Westminster Shorter Catechism (Q.4. "What is God?"). This answer reduces God to "dry bones," to abstract concepts. Theism betrays such fossilization. Theism outlines God philosophically. The biblical God cannot be contained by such theism or non-theism.

The non-theistic Conditional Arising and the Four Noble Truths hold humans responsible to the reality of the *continuity* of cause and effect. On the other hand, a God that is not bound by Conditional Arising brings a moment of *discontinuity* into ethical integrity. Divine discontinuity threatens our ethics. Since no one can tell when the discontinuity will take place, ethics always remains in a state of brokenness or incompleteness (1 Cor 4:5). The biblical word that replaces "discontinuity" is *pathos*. God is full of *pathos*. "My mind is turning over inside me. My emotions are agitated all together" (Hos 11:8, Anchor Bible Translation). Neither theism nor non-theism, but the God of *pathos* gives the distinctive mark to the Christian faith. What kind of *pathos*? It is a *pathos* overflowing with love and justice directed to our history.

149

In a striking contrast to Christianity, Buddhism, as has been pointed out, teaches no-self (*anatta*, translated in some Thai Buddhist literature as "ownerlessness") as the true identity of self. The *anatta* teaching, contrary to Christian interpretation, will not make us "dry bones" but "dancing bones." One must be free from the illusion of substantive self, says the Thai monastic monk, Buddhadasa Indapanno: "Anything in this world is perpetually flowing, forever breaking up, that is, it is impermanent. So we have to equip ourselves well with heedfulness. Don't go playing with those things! They will bite you. They will slap your face. They will bind and hold you fast. You will be made to sit and weep, or perhaps even to commit suicide. . . . Nothing whatsoever should be grasped at or clung to" (Bhikkhu, 1966, p. 5).

All in this world is perpetually flowing. It is the illusion of "I" and "my" that produces greed *(tanha)*. Buddhadasa continues: "Now it is usually proclaimed eloquently, also mistakenly and misleadingly, that birth, aging, and death are suffering. But birth is *not* suffering, aging is *not* suffering, death is *not* suffering in a case where there is no grasping at 'my' birth, 'my' aging, 'my' death. At the moment, we are grasping, regarding birth, aging, pain, and death as 'mine.' If we don't grasp, they are not suffering; they are only bodily changes" *(ibid.,* 51). "A mind is *empty* (or unencumbered, or disengaged, or free) when it is free of craving, aversion, and delusion" *(ibid.,* 30). Thus, belief in a personal self is at the heart of humankind's ethical malaise. This radical suggestion is rooted in the idea that everything in the world is in a state of constant change and flux. The ethical message of this is: "Do not be grasping"!

Is there, in Christian teaching, any such awareness of the "illusion of *I or my?"* The New Testament moves in that direction but from sociological and political angles. "You know that among the Gentiles those whom they recognize as their rulers lord it over them, and their great ones are tyrants over them. But it is not so among you; but whoever wishes to become great among you must be your servant, and whoever wishes to be first among you must be slave of all" (Mk 10:42-44).

Both Buddhist *dharma* and Christian theology oppose the inflation of self. (See Acts 12:22.) Christianity holds that the very concept of "I" is real and sacred; embodying the image of God, it is this "I" that can deny itself for the public good, and practice what is commanded by

Christ: "Go and do likewise" (Lk 10:37). I hold that the Buddhist concept of the "I" as a fetter does not necessarily quarrel with the Christian call: "Go and do likewise."

3. The Sangha Ethic

The English word "monk" or "monastery" etymologically implies "being alone." The Buddhist word *sangha* is a community of *bhikkhus* (monks). A *bhikkhu* is one who has placed himself under the rules of the *Sangha* (monastic community). Those rules are called *patimokkha*, which, in Thai Buddhism, number 227 precepts. Each *bhikkhu*, though, in the *sangha* is individually a "lone rhinoceros." *Patimokkha* is about *Adibrahmacarikasikkha* (the principal training in the pure life).

The first four of the 227 Precepts of the Thai Buddhism are a "Defeat Group." They prohibit (1) Sexual intercourse; (2) Taking anything worth more than five "masok" (about one baht) without the owner's consent; (3) Intentional murder; and (4) Falsely claiming the possession of the highest Truth of humankind. The monk who violates any one of these four is "defeated." After this most serious "Defeat Group" comes "the Formal Meeting Group" (of which precept 12 forbids "in revengeful anger falsely accusing another monk of an offense against any of the first four precepts,") and moving down through less serious offenses to the last group called "Training Rules Group," precepts 146 to 227. The spirit that guides the "principal training in the pure life" is summarized by precept 165 of the *Dhamma Pada*: "By oneself, indeed, is evil done; by oneself is one defiled; by oneself evil left undone; by oneself, indeed, is one purified. Purity and impurity depend on oneself. No one purifies another."

People must know that "no one purifies another." This is the way of the lone rhinoceros. In contrast to this, the more community-oriented Mahayana tradition says, "the Buddha will purify you." What are the social and political roles of the *sangha* ethics? How does this ethic promote abolition of wars, just distribution of wealth, eradication of racism and ethnic conflict? So far, the *nirvana*-oriented monastic Buddhism has done little to involve itself in these social issues. The dialogue between the two traditions, the monastic and the Mahayana, will strengthen Buddhist ethics. This dialogue will continue so long as all

Buddhists recognize the problem of human greed as primary. With this basic recognition, their ethics should move in the direction of "Eradication of poverty and creating employment opportunities, improving living standards, expanding education facilities, providing better health facilities, promotion of human rights, disarmament" (Pieris, 53).

4. The Royal View of Polity

One of the Hindu religious ideologies that impacted its far-reaching civilization is the idea of "incarnation" (avatar, "descent"). The Hindu world decided that the historical Buddha is an avatar of the eternal dharma. The idea of devarajah (god-king) has been supported by the avatar ideology. In Thailand the devarajah ideology has developed since the Sukithai kingdom of the thirteenth century. The king is understood to be an embodiment of the Buddhist dharma and the protector of the community of monks, the sangha. He is the link between the human and divine worlds. Cosmology and hierarchy find felicitous harmony in the person of the king. Modernization of Thai politics was achieved when this time-honored religio-political metaphysics showed the flexibility to accept a form of constitutional monarchy in 1932. Here the historical was united with the cosmological. In this unity is the secret of the enormous popularity of the present Buddhist king, Phumipol. The Thai popular attachment to the devarajah ideology has not disappeared even in the busy westernized life of Bangkok.

In Western Christian civilization the idea of the divine right of kings has been accosted by biblical hesitation. The king does not occupy the cosmological center or the hierarchical peak since cosmology is subordinated to theology ("God is the creator of the cosmos"). The invisible God, not king, represents the supreme authority. Hence the person of the king has been essentially downsized and demythologized. In confronting King David the prophet Nathan expressed the radical principle of modernization (2 Sam 12).

The Nathan episode takes us to a critical issue that perpetually faces humanity, i.e., the "boosting" of the conditional to the unconditional (Paul Tillich), from which all kinds of violence emanates. The logic and contents of primitive Buddhism's Conditional Arising and the

152

Four Noble Truths prevent this "boosting." At this critical point Christian theology meets the Buddhist *dharma*. The Buddhist observation of human existence cools the passion that fosters absolutization.

Officially the image of *devarajah* must symbolize both transcendental and temporal values, though the rich rituals that surround the king create a sense of incongruity between the *nirvana* ideal and the earthly glory of the *devarajah*. This has not become a serious problem; the cosmology of the Hindu-Buddhist world is relaxed compared to that of the Christian West, in which it is subordinated to the higher principle. The Buddhist mystery stays inside the cosmos, while the Christian mystery reaches outside the cosmos. The contrast is between cosmological mysticism and eschatological mysticism.

The prophetic religion of the Hebrew Bible warns of the lure of cosmological charms (Jer 7:18). The New Testament also warns of the pull of the "elemental spirit of the cosmos" (*stoicheia tou kosmou*, Gal 4:9). The primacy of *theos* over *kosmos* is foundational in biblical teaching. The essential Buddhism of the Conditional Arising warns against the charms of the cosmos. The Conditional Arising does not support the ideology of *devarajah* and of the *avatar*, of the cosmological scheme. Christianity speaks about the *avatar* in terms of "emptying" (*kenosis* Phil 2:7). It is a theological, not a cosmological, thought. Here Buddhism comes nearer to Christianity than Hinduism, which drinks heavily from the cosmic charms. Buddhism is less charmed than Hinduism by the cosmos, for the universal character of Buddhist ethics asserts that each individual — in this life, rather than a previous one — is responsible for his or her own life and future.

Christian theology appreciates Buddhist observation of human life. It realizes that the meaning of revelation which "flesh and blood" cannot reveal still has to dialogue with observation of human life such as that of Buddhism in order to find its place in human life. The *point* of revelation must become a part of the *line* of observation. Then the *line* would be criticized, expanded, and deepened for the benefit of universal ethics and ecumenical theology. In our globalized future, a major opportunity and challenge for the Christian church will be to enter into dialogue with Buddhists over these four major ethical issues and contrasts that I have described: the source of authority in religious beliefs and ethical norms, the nature and role of the "self" as an ethical agent, the importance of community in encouraging moral action, and the religious and ethical place of government.

Works Cited

Abe, Masao. *Zen and Western Thought.* 1985.

Buddhist Scriptures. Penguin Classics.

The Book of Kindred Sayings. The Pali Text Society, 1930.

The Dammapada.

De Silva, Lily. *Dialogue.* Colombo, Sri Lanka: The Ecumenical Institute, 1990.

Duncan, Ronald, ed. *Selected Writings of Mahatma Gandhi.* Fontana, 1972.

Pieris, Aloysius. *Dialogue.* Colombo, Sri Lanka: The Ecumenical Institute, 1986-87.

Indapanno, Buddhadasa. *Buddhist Dharma for Students.* Translated by Ariyananda Bhikkhu. Bangkok: Thammasat University, 1966.

Indapanno, Buddhadasa. *Christianity and Buddhism.* Sinclair Thompson Memorial Lecture. Bangkok, 1967.

Tillich, Paul. *Systematic Theology,* vol. 1. 1953.

Udana. Translated by Bhadragaka. Bangkok, 1954.

11

Muhammad's Significance for Christians: Some Personal Reflections

LAMIN SANNEH

Christians' attitude toward Islam can be greatly enhanced through a proper understanding of the place of Muhammad in Islam. Muhammad's authority is stamped on Islam in a decisive way, leaving Islam as a religion of profound personal agency and commitment. Though later Muslim authorities spoke of the religion as *din al-fitr*, "natural religion," meaning religion as psychological inevitability, and inscribed as such into humanity's natural constitution, the fact remains that the Prophet's personal example confirmed Islam as something fit for personal decision and choice. There subsists throughout the centuries of development and expansion in Islam this decisive call to the individual, a call that originated with the call of the Prophet himself and has ever since been repeated in the multiple daily call of the muezzin. The ethical imperatives of personal commitment, what the Qur'an states as the central concept of *'ibadah*, human servanthood, are non-negotiable. In the final analysis Muhammad's personal example is decisive, and Islam remains a matter of universal personal conviction.

Consequently, although Muhammad lived a long time ago, he remains a living presence. If Muhammad is remote, it is remoteness of historical uniqueness, not of metaphysical difference from us. He is ex-

This paper is adapted from my book, *Piety and Power: Muslims and Christians in West Africa* (Maryknoll, NY: Orbis Books, 1996).

alted in his humanity, not in spite of it. Muhammad's person became the subject of rich religious feeling, the channel that received and refined an immense outpouring of spiritual tribute. His birth, for example, has the element of the marvelous all around it. A typical account speaks of how the thrones of royalty were all overturned, the idols of heathendom fell on their faces, the wild animals of East and West as well as creatures of the sea prophesied good tidings when the happy news of his birth was announced. His mother was told in a dream to call him Muhammad because his final reward will be praised (Ar. *ahmad*).

There is little doubt about Muhammad's biographical preeminence in the hearts and minds of Muslims. Carlyle was right in this sense to fix on him human distinction. "They called him Prophet, you say? Why, he stood there face to face with them; bare, not enshrined in any mystery; visibly clouting his own cloak, cobbling his own shoes; fighting, counseling, ordering in the midst of them: they must have seen what kind of man he *was*, let him be *called* what you like! No emperor with his tiaras was obeyed as this man in a cloak of his own clouting."

In the very things that Christians find tedious and monotonous in the repetitive details of Muhammad's life Muslims find reason for confidence. Muhammad for them is not the thinker who produces abstract systems of thought proving his case by logical demonstration. Rather, Muhammad is rooted in the very substance of time and space. His voice vibrates throughout the range of Muslim life and action, his outward manner and demeanor the very meaning of inward *barakah*. It is this *externality* of Muhammad, that is to say, his embodied presence, that demonstrates to Muslims the validity of the truth he proclaimed. Muhammad's historical concreteness is thus the close-knit fabric with which Muslims clothe the divine injunctions. Thus otherwise mundane acts like washing, cutting one's nails and hair, eating, marrying and raising a family, greeting people, selling and buying, and so forth, carry unique merit in the particular setting of the Prophet's life. He made *barakah* live.

Consequently, Muslims have available to them a rich source of biographical detail on the Prophet's life, the source we know as *hadith*. Through its formal stylized channel Muhammad's historical concreteness is conveyed in the copious flow of anecdote, episode, and reminiscence. Often the chains of transmission are so thick with names of witnesses and raconteurs that the substance of what is reported is disproportionately slight, causing us to wonder why a lone night-fly might be worth the elaborate day-long industry of the spider's web. Yet it would be wrong to judge the *hadith* solely by the rules of critical abundance. The *hadith* presents Muhammad not just as one who spoke but as one who was also spoken for by others. We have in the *hadith* not just one biography but innumerable biographies, or else biographical vignettes and cues, what the science of *hadith* calls *'ilm al-rijal*. *Hadith* becomes an exemplary channel, a vessel that drips with what is contained in it, as al-Chazali would say. Men and women who would otherwise be inconsequential by the rules of historical grandeur arrive in our company as witnesses, or witnesses of the witnesses of Muhammad.

The track by which biography proceeds depends, then, on the repeatability of biographical example, so that an idea or practice is attached to the tone, a face, and a gesture. The soundness of the chain of transmission turns almost exclusively on the trustworthiness of the links of witnesses, with the slight danger of distortion occurring, either because an otherwise worthy-sounding account fails by its weak link, or a spurious tradition slips through by being predicated of a recognized name. While clearly depending on the memory of real persons, biographical reminiscence may, therefore, complicate the historical record, leaving us uncertain about the extent of motivated intervention in the handing down of tradition. It is to this phenomenon that scholars like Wensinck, Goldziher, and Schacht have called our attention.

Truth and Ordinariness

As in the financial world, so here also counterfeits need the original to succeed, and it is above all the genuine article of Muhammad's life that has been both curb and incentive for over-imaginativeness. Muhammad so dominated his age that he became its symbol and ideal. He is presented in such tireless detail and depicted with such unforgettable repetition, and his name is so highly revered in the devotional cycle, that concern with his biography animates the whole landscape of religious and historical understanding. On every detail of routine and personal style, alike on circumstances and persons, Muhammad alights as precept and principle.

If the pious disciples embellished Muhammad's biography, they have not done so completely at the expense of the commonplace. That commonplace concerns the ordinary and natural character of his birth and upbringing, a character still preserved in the oldest records we possess, and that, furthermore, survives in all mature reflections of his *sunnah*.

Virtually all Muslim authors on the subject stick more or less to the following outline. Muhammad was born in about A.D. 570, the exact date not being certain. His parents were Aminah and 'Abdallah; his father died before Muhammad was born, and his mother when the child was six. Muhammad was raised by a wet nurse, Halimah. Muhammad was placed under the care of his grandfather, 'Abdul Muttalib, who died when Muhammad was eight. Then he was handed over to Abu Talib, his uncle and the father of 'Alf, the future fourth caliph. Thus, as sura 93 points out, God found Muhammad an "orphan *(yatim)* and succored him, enriched and guided him." Pious tradition went on to add a colorful flourish to the detail by regarding him as the *yatimah*, the pearl of priceless worth, as Annemarie Schimmel has pointed out.

As a young boy Muhammad engaged in trade, accompanying his uncle, Abu Talib, in the Syrian caravan trade. On one such trip he encountered a monk, Bahira, who recognized the seal of prophethood between the child's shoulders. Muslim accounts speak of Bahira as testifying to Muhammad's future stature as the prophet foretold in John's Gospel, the reference being to the "Comforter" that Jesus promised his own disciples (Jn 14:1-7, 26). That has become a source of much interest among Muslims and controversy with Christians. Muhammad was then aged twelve.

At age twenty-five Muhammad married Khadijah, the woman who had employed him in her caravan trade, at her instigation. The marriage was reward for Muhammad's honesty, though she was fifteen years his senior. She bore him four daughters, and a son or two who died in infancy. Khadijah was a tower of strength to Muhammad, putting the weight of wealth and experience behind him. Thus when Muhammad was going through a dark night of the soul, with great doubts gnawing at his resolve, it was Khadijah who acted to steady his will and calm his nerve. He used to retire to the hills surrounding Mecca to meditate privately. That was the setting in which he received the call to prophethood.

Yet much ambiguity surrounds the actual details of the call. Two versions are combined in the standard account of Ibn Ishaq (d. A.D. 768). In one strand of the account Muhammad receives a vision at night in an unlit cave, and is summoned to recite the words of the revelations, those being the opening words of sura 96. This strand contains what some scholars believe to be a case of special pleading by those with an exegetical ax to grind, namely, the wish to promote sura 96 to the first place of the Qur'an because of the sura's inaugural word in the imperative mood: *iqra*, "recite," is a cognate of the verbal noun "Qur'an," "recital." In the other strand, a vision comes to him in daylight, or at least when the "clear horizon" (of sura 81:19) is glanced by the light of the rising sun as he stood on the open hills. This incident is described in sura 53, the sura with famous *satanic verses*. Among other things, the sura speaks of a divine or celestial being who stood in the highest part of the horizon and approached to a distance of "two bows, or even closer," before revealing the matter to the Prophet.

Whether in the strand with the unlit cave or with that of the clear horizon, the accounts represent Muhammad as having a frightful time of it. "Sometimes the Revelation comes like the sound of a bell," he testified. "That is the most painful way. When it ceases I have remembered what was said. Sometimes it is an angel who talks like a human, and I remember what he says."

As closely examined by W. Montgomery Watt in his two-volume biography of the Prophet, the early preaching of Muhammad was taken up with the themes of resurrection and judgment, of a fierce eschatological eruption that would leave no one unanswerable, though faithful Muslims would abide its terror and receive the divine reward. There is a strong eschatological seriousness about the Meccan phase of Mohammed's preaching. In later revelations, especially those occurring at Medina, the tone shifts, to administrative questions and individual and collective guidelines, such as happens when religious protest has acquired the power to impose its will.

At any rate, at Mecca Muhammad came into conflict with the leading citizens, who perceived him as a threat and a social upstart. For about a decade, from 610 to 619, Muhammad continued to receive revelations until he was able to gather a fairly sizable number of followers. In 619 he lost Khadijah through death, and in similar fashion his uncle, Abu Talib. They were indispensable pillars of his movement and a source of personal strength and inspiration. Their deaths affected him deeply and exposed him even more to his Meccan antagonists. In 621 Muhammad was approached by a party of sympathizers from Yathrib, an agricultural settlement to the north, lying on the sensitive artery that carried the caravan trade with Syria. These sympathizers appealed to him to come to Yathrib to help mediate in their internal quarrels — in effect, asking him to take over leadership of their community. With the circle of hostility narrowing around him in Mecca, Muhammad responded eagerly, if cautiously, to their overture; he did not want a premature leak of his plans to arouse Meccan hostility. He sent some of his Meccan followers ahead of him while he made secret preparations to leave with Abu Bakr, an early convert and one destined to succeed the Prophet as caliph. Yathrib was to be renamed "the city of the Prophet," *madinatu-n-nabi,* shortened to Madina or Medina.

The propitious historical circumstance of the transfer to Medina has in retrospect afforded lavish incentive for pious legend. One such legend recounts how after Muhammad and Abu Bakr had taken refuge in a cave en route to Medina, a spider spun its web and pigeons built their nests over it as evidence of miraculous intervention to shield the pair from the pursuing Meccans, a pursuit referred to in the Qur'an (sura 9:40). Eventually Muhammad reached Medina in September 622. The Muslim party he had sent out had preceded him in the city, arriving there in June of the same year. The Islamic calendar observes June 622 as year one of the *hijrah,* i.e., the emigration from Mecca, for although the Prophet left Mecca later, the decision to do so had been made.

Soon after arriving in Medina Muhammad promulgated a constitution in an effort to govern the place. In the constitution he offered protection and security to the warring tribes living there, including a sizable Jewish community. The Muslims introduced a new element of social stratification, one based not on blood and kindred solidarity, but on religion and obedience to the Prophet. At the top of the social order was the Prophet himself, followed by his companions *(ashab),* the ranks of emigrants *(muhajirun),* the Medinan helpers *(ansar),* the tributary populations, captives taken in raids and similar sources, and those waiting to be subdued. Such were the delineations of the new Pax Islamica: at Medina Muhammad thus became both his own St. Paul and Constantine, a double role that left Islam a religion and a state.

Mecca continued to resist Muhammad, and he for his part could not rest until he had annexed it to his purpose. In 624, in a famous battle that took place at Badr near Medina, the Muslim forces, surprised and outnumbered, overcame enormous odds to break up the Meccan lines and put the enemy to flight. Badr was celebrated as a miraculous victory, the Qur'an referring to it as the time when God acted by the hands of the faithful Muslims to assure success. "Not you cast when you cast," it affirmed, "but God cast" (sura 8:17). The victory at Badr joined the military function to the prophetic one, and set it up as the consecrated partner of the higher oracle.

Perhaps success went to the heads of the victors, for next year saw them in another battle with the Meccans, at Mt. Uhud; this time the Muslims suffered serious losses. Some of the prophet's best soldiers were lost in action, though he himself escaped with his life. He lost two teeth and sustained an injury in his left foot.

In 627 the Meccans tried again to storm Medina but were repulsed. The following year the Prophet decided to perform the *haji*, pilgrimage, to the Ka'aba which, since about 623 or 624, had replaced Jerusalem as the *qiblah*, the direction for the prescribed prayers of salat. Though he did not that year perform the *haji* he concluded a treaty with the now pacified Meccans, who recognized his right of access to the Ka'aba. It was a matter of time before he took Mecca itself, which he did without contest in 630. He proceeded to clean out the Ka'aba of all its idols and sacred images and he reconsecrated it to Muslim service. He then returned to Medina.

After Khadijah died he married several times, including 'A'fsha, a young virgin and a favorite wife of his, widows of soldiers who had died in battle, and Zynab, the ex-wife of his adopted son, Zayd. A Coptic slave girl who was given to the Prophet bore him a son who died before he was two. His wives were respectfully called "the mothers of the faithful" (sura 33:6). After his death they were allowed to remarry (33:53).

In 632 Muhammad again made the *haji* to Mecca from Medina. It turned out to be his farewell pilgrimage. According to standard exegesis, he received confirmation of his mission on that occasion when God assured him: *inni akmaltu laka dinkika Islam dinan.* "I have perfected for you Islam your religion" (5:5). On 8 June 632 Muhammad died in 'A'fsha's apartments. 'A'fsha was then aged 18. His burial site was called Rawdah, "the green," the mausoleum in Medina that pilgrims visit, saying, "I bear witness that thou art the Apostle of God. Thou hast conveyed the message. Thou hast fulfilled the trust. Thou hast counseled the community and enlightened the gloom, and shed glory on the darkness, and uttered words of wisdom."

Abu Bakr's assurance to the grief-stricken Muslims that although Muhammad was dead, yet God lives has served the cause more than he intended, for it is precisely in the assurance that God lives that Muhammad has found room to proliferate in the devotions and allegiance of Muslims the world over. Thus in the great monotheist witness of the faithful the name of the Prophet is joined to that of God, and Muhammad becomes the gateway to monotheist fidelity. Muslims might forgive anyone for taking the name of God lightly, but not so the name of Muhammad. We evade the Muslim sense of religious truth if we avoid the figure of the Prophet in the mistaken belief that it is God alone who matters. God has in Muhammad everything God must have in earthly or heavenly company, so that any attempt to force a general, unspecific mandate on God is to presume inexcusably on Muhammad's historical commission. Muslims feel that insofar as we are concerned as human beings, Muhammad is necessary and essential to participation in the divine scheme for human life. The Prophet is the indispensable guarantor of Islam's particularity, for it is he who prevents Islam's being ground into a general and inoffensive religious blend.

The Spiritual Heritage

Muhammad was called *uswa hasana* (33:21), "the beautiful model," his followers believing that God had sent him "as a mercy for the worlds" *(rahmatan li-l-'alamin)*, and that God and His angels pronounce blessings on him (33:56). The worlds of the Qur'an might be those of Muhammad himself: "Lo, as for me, my Lord has guided me unto a straight path, a right religion, the community of Abraham, the upright, who was no idolater. Say: Lo, my worship and my sacrifice and my living and my dying are for God, Lord of the worlds" (sura 6:162).

In the *shahadah*, the "witness," Muhammad's name is invoked to give its distinctive monotheist flavor. As Wilfred Smith has rightly observed, the reference to Muhammad in the *shahadah* is not so much a reference about him as an individual per se as it is about his role as the bearer of revelation: Muhammad becomes in effect "an aspect of God's activity." It is the same idea that has permitted Muhammad to become normative for Muslim life and conduct down through the ages.

A modern commentator has written, "For Muslims the moral and spiritual worth of the Prophet is not an abstraction or supposition; it is a lived reality, and is precisely this which proves its authenticity retrospectively." The founder of Islamic jurisprudence, al-Shafii, had pioneered a revolutionary legal methodology by establishing the *sunnah* of the Prophet as a canonical source. He built the immense structure of Islamic classical law on that single foundation, an achievement that has continued to affect all subsequent development of the law. At a less technical level, the words of al-Ghazali (1058-1111) illustrate what practical lessons might be derived from what is judged authentic in the biography of Muhammad. He wrote in his *magnum opus*, the *al-Ihya 'Ulum Din* (20th chapter) thus:

> Know that the key to happiness is to follow the sunna and to imitate the Messenger of God in all his coming and going, his movements and rest, in his way of eating, his attitude, his sleep and his talk. I do not mean this in regard to religious observance, for there is no reason to neglect the traditions which were concerned with this aspect. I rather mean all the problems of custom and usage; for only by following them unrestricted succession is possible. God has said: "Say: if you love God, follow me, and God will love you" (sura 3:29), and He has said: "What the messenger has brought — accept it, and what he has prohibited — refrain from it!" (sura 59:7). That means, you have to sit while putting on trousers, and to stand when winding a turban, and to begin with the right foot when putting on shoes. . . .

It would be both unrealistic and facile to call for duplication within historic Christianity of the *sunnah* theme of Islam, though Butler's *Lives of the Saints* evokes the feeling. Yet a close consideration of the

Muslim attitude to biography should challenge any lingering suspicion that lived reality can be only a subversion of the truth and a distraction from history.

Second, we should be imaginative enough to appreciate what Muhammad means to Muslims rather than persisting with the delusion that if we remain adamant long enough in our repudiation, especially when supported with historical-critical claims, Muslim confidence will crumble. Whatever such an attitude might imply about the transitoriness of Muslim claims, stubbornness is not a single-edged weapon of religious combat. Both sides know well enough the coarse marks that crusaders' chain mail cut in each other's collective memory, for every time we hear the rattle of name-calling or the stampede of exclusivism, we open wounds with the crude clamps of that earlier age. It does not require any generosity of spirit to meet each other under that weight.

Third, as we enter the twenty-first century we would do well to learn from Muslims how religion and politics, church and state, the private and public have much to do with each other. The fact that Muhammad combined in his own person the functions of St. Paul and Constantine gives Muslims an important premise of religious participation in the world. Muslims understand better than Christians the significance of religion not just as something we *think* about — not just as a cognitive affair — but as something we *act* on and *act out*.

Freedom of religion in the West has tended to mean freedom to think what we like, rather than freedom to *act* according to religious teachings. We are, for example, free to love our neighbor as ourselves provided it is the neighbor as defined by our neighborhood, race, or class, rather than the neighbor defined as the child of God without the presumption of national or cultural qualifications. There are, of course, immense problems in joining religion to politics, however warily it is done, but there would appear to be even greater dangers in driving an absolute wedge between them, which only incites a frenzy of political self-absolutization — and a corresponding moral reductionism. The modern secular disenchantment shows that "man cannot live by bread alone," and that spiritual values are critical to responsible stewardship.

That was the theme of Vaclav Havel in his address on January 21, 1990, to the Senate of the United States during his official visit to Washington, D.C., though the American media omitted all such reference. In words that recall Muhammad's challenge to the Meccan materialism of his day, Havel challenged his audience:

> the most dangerous enemy today is no longer the dark forces of to- talitarianism, the various hostile and plotting mafias, but our own bad qualities. My presidential program is, therefore, to bring spiri- tuality, moral responsibility, humanness, and humility into politics and, in that respect, to make clear that there is something higher above us, that our deeds do not disappear into the black hole of time but are recorded somewhere and judged, that we have neither the right nor a reason to think we understand everything and that we can do everything.

What Havel identifies as secular self-sufficiency Muslims attack as *shirk*, the false absolutes of human idolatry. It is time we realized that truth is not a matter of individual convenience.

Finally, to bring the discussion into line with some Christian reflec- tions, we in the West can learn a lot about ourselves as we attempt to understand how for Muslims Muhammad's life and example constitute the source and legitimization of reform: Islam was born in the Prophet's *hijrah* even though Muslims also believe it was conceived in heaven. For its part, the church was born at Pentecost whence it became a thorough- going Gentile movement. After Pentecost Christianity became a reli- gious movement on the peripheries of Bethlehem and Jerusalem as Christian communities sprang up in Antioch, Ephesus, Philippi, Cor- inth, Thessalonica, Athens, Rome, Alexandria, and beyond. If the *hijrah* confirmed and preserved the Arabicness of Islam, and, within that, the indispensable universality of Mecca and Medina, Pentecost, by contrast, allowed the church to dispense altogether with the original Aramaic and Hebrew of Jesus' preaching, and, with that, Jerusalem as an exclusive center for orthodoxy, and to embrace languages and cultures hitherto considered alien to the law and the prophets.

The *hijrah* ensconced Islam in the birthplace of Muhammad, and even Shi'ite separatism has not challenged that. Through the steady eye of the *hijrah* the camel of world Islam has been made to pass, however uneven or slow the pace of orthodox conformity. The *hijrah* has furnished the written charter for the reform of local Muslim practice, from Sinkiang in China to Sine-Saloum in Senegambia.

The opportunity for mutual instruction exists in the fact that Muslims and Christians have strengths and weaknesses which contrast with each other. The Arabicity of Islam, expressed in the nontranslatable Qur'an, enables the religion to enter local cultures in order finally to transcend them and give them decisive Meccan orientation. That Islam has more or less succeeded in this, where it has succeeded at all, amounts to a considerable achievement. That has been its strength. By contrast, the fact that at least in its modern expansion Christianity through vernacular translations of the scriptures has consecrated the indigenous medium also attests to its strength in linking its spread to vernacular creativity. And therein lie also their respective weaknesses. By establishing vernacular translation into a principle of religious conversion, Christians have unleashed all the consequences of local rivalry and schism, whereas by adhering to the rule of nontranslatability, Muslims have disenfranchised the vernacular as canonical medium, and thus suppressed a unique and indispensable source of indigenous vitality.

Speaking for the Christian side, we ought to reaffirm with as much confidence as is consistent with our history of cultural imperialism the essentially Gentile character of the church, a character stamped upon it by the Spirit itself. The Pentecostal insight continues to have revolutionary implications for interreligious as well as cross-cultural understanding. The fact of the matter is that the disciples were in no doubt that Gentile Antioch had just as exalted a place in God's scheme as Jerusalem, and that all hitherto taboo cultures and peoples stand fully and unconditionally admitted into the fellowship — that the native idioms, until then regarded as unworthy, were henceforth consecrated to bear the full and authentic message of God's forgiveness.

All this revolutionary conception of religious truth was made possible by the suffering, death, and resurrection of Jesus Christ, the One who redeems us and our cultural worlds from the stigma of all untouchability. Our difference with Muslims on this point must not be overlooked. The nontranslatability of the Qur'an does not deny the significance of language and culture, only that it assigns to the untranslated scripture an ontological priority of exclusiveness, whereas Christian translatability concedes an identical significance for language and culture by the radically different procedure of pluralist inclusiveness. Just as Muslims find it difficult to conceive of monotheist truth apart from Muhammad's unique and personal mediation, so Christians find it hard to conceive of a redeemed world without the agency of God effected in Christ.

12

The New Ecumenism

CECIL M. ROBECK, JR.

As the twentieth century races rapidly towards its conclusion, there are several facts worth noting that have implications for ecumenism. First, the church has now existed for two millennia. During its first millennium its members contended repeatedly with one another to guarantee at least the veneer of unity. To be sure, there were some very significant differences between churches in the East and churches in the West. But in the midst of that diversity, because both heresy and schism were taken so seriously, there was unity between them. All parts of the church were essentially in full communion with every other part of the church, and thereby, with the whole church. That all came crashing to an end in A.D. 1054, with a massive political, theological, and cultural separation of East and West.

Second, the second millennium has been marked more by division than by unity. Following the break between East and West, the West, in particular, has continued to be plagued by schism. The emergence then rejection of various renewal (e.g., Waldensian) and later Reformation movements, denies any genuine claim to Roman catholicity. Luther, Zwingli, the Anabaptists, Calvin, and even Henry VIII all broke ranks with Rome over significant issues. The compromise policy of *cuius regio, eius religio*, while helpful in bringing about a religious truce of sorts, ultimately guaranteed further divisions along national, cultural, and linguistic lines. As the church was transplanted onto the missionary soils of the New World, as well as Asia and Africa, it resulted in yet more divisions. New denominations (e.g., Cumberland Presbyterians, Free Will Baptists, Reformed Church in America), church families (e.g., Adventists), and traditions (e.g., Pentecostalism) came into being. Concern over institutionalism, clericalism, doctrinal purity, and other issues have given rise to other denominations as well.

The twentieth century will undoubtedly go into the history books with two major notations. First, it was the century in which the churches became concerned once again about the visible unity of the church. That fact became apparent through (1) the famous 1910 Edinburgh missionary conference, (2) the 1920 encyclical issued by the Ecumenical Patriarchate, and (3) the formation of the World Council of Churches. Second, it was the century in which the church rediscovered the Holy Spirit. This fact has been evidenced in (1) the rise of the modern Pentecostal movement, (2) its appearance within the historic churches in the form of charismatic renewal, and (3) the emergence of Vatican Council II in response to the prayer of John XXIII for a "New Pentecost."

The formal ecumenical hope of the church worldwide reached its zenith in the third quarter of the twentieth century. The World Council of Churches held its first Assembly in Amsterdam in 1948. The Orthodox entered fully into these discussions in 1961. And the Vatican held its pace-setting Council between 1962 and 1965. Indeed, the years between 1948 and 1965 were heady ecumenical years. Churches were full and parishioners were filled with hope. The East and West were once again talking to one another. The churches of the Reformation, many of their offspring, and the ancient churches of the East and West began to discover one another.

During the past twenty-five years, many of the earlier ecumenical hopes have gone unfulfilled. To be sure, a number of fruitful bilateral and multilateral discussions are still under way. And the past twenty-five years have seen some significant intra-confessional headings such as the mergers that have occurred among Presbyterians and Lutherans in the United States. Several united or uniting churches have been formed in Canada, Australia, Great Britain, Indonesia, and elsewhere. The Consultation on Church Union (COCU) has apparently finally negotiated its long and rocky road to some sense of completion. But for many, the pace of formal ecumenical successes has diminished to such an extent that they wonder whether the churches are not now at an impasse.

Many of the historic churches that worked to achieve some level of visible unity have seen massive declines in their membership as well as their influence over the past quarter century. We have watched as the National Council of Churches of Christ in the United States of America has undergone reorganization after reorganization. The World Council of Churches has laid off over half of its staff within the past decade even as it has attempted to establish a new "Common Vision and Understanding" for its role in the world. In spite of the publication of the *Decree on Ecumenism* and Pope John Paul II's attempt to rearticulate the Vatican's commitment to ecumenism in his 1995 encyclical *Ut Unum Sint*, some critics have speculated on the extent to which the Roman Catholic Church seems to be backing away from its prior commitments on the subject.

We have watched, with interest, the exercise of muscle by the Patriarch of Moscow against "intruding" churches of the West as well as the Ecumenical Patriarchate, and we have been intrigued by the political posturing that Orthodox Archbishop Iakovos undertook in the United States shortly before his retirement. We have also seen the growing dissidence within denominations and church families over certain moral issues such as sexuality, which threaten still further what unity the churches have worked so hard to maintain. As a result of these struggles, some have argued that we have entered an "ecumenical winter" while others have suggested that perhaps some things may need to die in order for something new to arise from the ashes. (Heim, 1993, pp. 333-35)

In spite of all this turmoil, there have been signs of hope that something new may be on the way. Its emergence may shake the status quo to its very foundation, bringing in its wake a totally new way of thinking about such things. Many have been the calls for a "new ecumenism," one in which all Christians are able to sit at a table together, a table currently enjoyed by only certain Christians. In 1988, Professor Donald W. Dayton wrote a much-discussed essay titled "Yet Another Layer of the Onion: Or Opening the Ecumenical Door to Let the Riffraff In." In this thought-provoking article, he challenged the World Council of Churches to reassess its Reformed paradigm and make space for the Wesleyan-Holiness movement and Pentecostals. (Dayton, 87-100)

170

In 1992, Father Avery Dulles, S.J., summoned Roman Catholics to explore what he called "an ecumenism of mutual enrichment." The time is ripe, he argued,

> to welcome the more traditional and conservative churches into di-
> alogue. For the Catholic Church it may not prove easy to reach a
> consensus with either the Orthodox or the conservative Evangeli-
> cals, but these churches and communities may have more to offer
> than some others because they have dared to be different. Catholics
> have the right and duty to challenge the adequacy of some of their
> positions, but they should be invited to challenge Catholics in their
> turn. (Dulles, 1992, p. 193)

In 1996, Father O. C. Edwards, an Episcopalian, looked beyond the limits of the current membership of the National Council of Churches and argued that it should pursue Roman Catholics, Evangelicals, and Pentecostals as potential partners in its work. (Edwards, 1996, pp. 7-29) Later that year, the American Baptist theologian Mark Heim contended that both the National and World Councils of Churches needed to look beyond their declining vision, declining membership, and current financial predicaments. They needed to look at the places where the most dynamic growth was occurring, "among Pentecostals, Roman Catholics, Southern Baptists and independent churches." He went on to suggest that the very survival of ecumenism depends upon the inclusion of those who have traditionally been absent from the table, including Roman Catholics and Evangelicals of all stripes. (Heim, 1996, p. 780)

As early as the Canberra Assembly in 1991, the World Council of Churches saw the handwriting on the wall. That Assembly passed a ten-point proposal that outlined its concern to broaden the table in favor of Pentecostals. Since that time it has opened an Office of Church and Ecumenical Relations and actively pursued a number of regional and international consultations in which those who have traditionally not been at the table have been asked to participate. In his book *To Be the Church*, Konrad Raiser asked the question "Should the WCC therefore adjust or change its organizational structure to facilitate the full participation of these (non-member) churches?" (Raiser, 1997, p. 102) His response was that perhaps what was needed was something that operates at the international level with representation from "families of churches." Without using this specific terminology, the World Council of Churches' new policy statement on "Common Understanding and Vision" pursues this line of reasoning. It calls for the continuation of efforts to find "new forms of relationships at all levels between WCC member churches, other churches and other ecumenical organizations." (WCC, Sept. 1997, p. 24)

If members of the World Council of Churches have begun to understand that genuine ecumenism can take place only when all players are at the table, another phenomenon has been equally interesting. It is the path of discovery that has led a number of Evangelicals, Charismatics, and Pentecostals to attempt to re-form their center or to seek out the more historic churches. Whether they be *Evangelicals on the Canterbury Trail*, as Wheaton theology professor Robert Webber has described those who have converted to the Anglican community; or they follow the lead of former Campus Crusade for Christ staffer Peter E. Gillquist, and are *Becoming Orthodox*; or they are like the many graduates of Gordon-Conwell Theological Seminary who have recently been celebrated for their conversion to the Roman Catholic Church, the message is the same. Christians are realizing they need more than they have been receiving in spiritual isolation from the rest of the church.

Each year I ask my students how many of them are still members of the denomination of their birth. Each year the number seems to drop. Each year I ask my students how many denominations they have joined. Each year the number seems to climb. Denominational loyalty is rare these days. The walls of partition are falling. Some of the transitions can be traced, undoubtedly, to the changes in the culture around us. Some of it can be traced to what might be described as a form of "grassroots" ecumenism. It is not always or often well thought out. It is not always for the best reasons. It may be sloppy. But it is real, nonetheless.

Some of these changes have come as a result of things like the impact of the Holy Spirit in charismatic renewal. Some have come as a result of participation in vital experiences of social activism, in CROP Walks or participation in Habitat for Humanity. Whatever we may think of mass movements such as Promise Keepers, they seem to have tapped into the spiritual yearnings and social identity issues of their participants. These movements, too, have served to break down previously existing walls between Christians. Calls for pluralism in the broader society and calls for wider religious denominational toleration from our various religious leaders have also played a role. The increasing reality of marriages to those in other faith traditions, the leveling effect of "Christian" television "churches" and televangelists, and increasing skepticism about inherited religious dogmas and ecclesiastical institutions, as well as personal quests for greater spirituality, have all contributed to these transitions as well. If we go by the signs around us, spiritual hunger is at an all-time high. Almost any attempt to offer or explain the supernatural, on the big screen or the television screen and as long as it is not traditional, is guaranteed to draw an audience.

Quite apart from the recent public discussions of the self-inflicted personal and political troubles of President Clinton, calls for civil decency, moral leadership, and greater character are on the rise. These calls have crossed all kinds of traditional lines, and may also be said to contribute to new forms of grassroots ecumenism. It is important to note that although the recent Lambeth Conference is merely advisory (it has no legislative authority), the Anglican bishops of the so-called "two-thirds world" sent a loud message to their British, European, and American counterparts on issues of sexuality, in spite of the fact that they were publicly ridiculed as backward and "superstitious." Their vote condemned homosexual practice as incompatible with the Bible, and called for greater sexual integrity. What is significant about this vote, besides the wide margin of its passage (526 to 70, with 45 abstentions), is that it is far more representative of the traditions not currently at most ecumenical tables than it is of the stereotypes that persist regarding WCC member churches.

This vote may not be popular with veteran ecumenists from more liberal traditions, though their "spin doctors" seem to miss the point. For the most part, as Avery Dulles has noted, they are those "with the least demanding doctrinal and liturgical heritage" (Dulles, 1992, p. 193), a heritage that does not necessarily hold the best solutions to many contemporary problems. Furthermore, the evangelical and charismatic wings of most historic denominations within the formal ecumenical movement, as well as others that Dulles describes as holding "firm doctrinal standards and stable traditions" *(ibid.)* have been grossly underrepresented at most "ecumenical" tables. Why they are underrepresented is surely the result of one or another of two possibilities.

It may be that those who are officially responsible for the ecumenical concerns of the historic Protestant churches, that is, certain denominational leaders and their ecumenical officers and their staffs, have purposely marginalized the concerns of those with whom they personally disagree: namely, the Evangelicals and Charismatics in their midst. Thus, the issue may be one in which certain denominational leaders as well as ecumenists are now being called to account for what amounts to a lack of accountability to the people they theoretically represent.

The argument may also go in another direction altogether: it may signal the lack of concern that Evangelicals and Charismatics have had for traditional forms of ecumenism. They have marginalized themselves by refusing to participate with those with whom they disagree, viewing such participation as compromise. In either case — and there is surely truth to be found in both positions — such disparate positions taken by people within the same camp suggests that no one is really listening to what the other is saying.

This vote may also reveal two other important facts about new ecumenical possibilities. First, new possibilities for convergence seem to be emerging, not merely and exclusively between churches that have historically participated in the National and World Councils of Churches, but between some of these churches and those who have not traditionally taken part. The first place this convergence exists, and where new relationships may develop, I think, may be between the Evangelical, Wesleyan-Holiness, Pentecostal, Roman Catholic, Orthodox, and missionary-planted historic Anglican and Protestant churches. Can you imagine an international community or forum in which these parties held the advantage? Would you or your denomination participate in such a community forum?

Second, and more important, Evangelicals, Pentecostals, Roman Catholics, Orthodox, and the overwhelming majority of believers in the "two-thirds world" are beginning to find one another. They are beginning to find common cause in spite of their apparent differences. And if their numbers mean anything, they may well be led in the future by those who have traditionally been underrepresented in all ecumenical discussions, those in the so-called "two-thirds world." What will the church sound like when the Christians of the Southern Hemisphere rise up to take their place as leaders of the world's Christians? How comfortable will you be in such a mix? Do you believe your personal interests would be well represented by them, or would you need to change, merely to find acceptance among those you now call "sister" or "brother"?

Since 1972 an international discussion has been going on between the Pontifical Council for Promoting Christian Unity, the Vatican, and a number of Pentecostal denominations and leaders. Its most recent work on "Evangelization, Proselytism, and Common Witness" has received good marks from observers in the secular and religious press alike. This work is being done with integrity, and it is being discussed positively in the larger church world. As a result, leaders in both camps are being forced to take this work more seriously than at any time in the past, even if they are not yet in a position to support it openly.

Similarly, from 1977 to 1984, the Pontifical Council met with a range of Evangelical leaders on the subject of mission. (Meeking and Stott, 1986) This conversation was renewed in 1991 with representatives from the World Evangelical Fellowship. A monthly dialogue between Evangelicals and Roman Catholics has been co-sponsored by Fuller Theological Seminary and the Archdiocese of Los Angeles since 1987, also with good results. One cannot help but notice the amount of discussion that has emerged around the *Evangelicals and Catholics Together* project of Evangelical Charles Colson and recent Lutheran-turned-Roman Catholic, Fr. Richard John Neuhaus (Colson and Neuhaus, 1995). Still other discussions have been held since 1995 between Evangelicals and the Orthodox churches, some of them facilitated by the World Council of Churches. At the present time, there is also considerable discussion over the possibility that, in light of the changes in Central and Eastern Europe and the former Soviet Union, similar discussions might be pursued between Pentecostals and the Orthodox.

What all of these facts suggest for the future of ecumenism, or "The New Ecumenism," is that ecumenism will continue to be transformed in the foreseeable future. If there has been a failure at the official and formal level of ecumenical discussion, we have seen significant movement, indeed, encouraging signs at the grassroots level. Professor George Lindbeck's observations seem quite appropriate:

> Unitive ecumenism, among other things, needs to be reconceived. It can no longer be thought of, as I have done most of my life, as a matter of reconciling relatively intact and structurally still-Constantinian communions from the top down. Rather it must be thought of as reconstituting Christian community and unity from, so to speak, the bottom up. The ecumenical journey when thus conceived will be longer but also more adventurous: renewal and unification become inseparable. (Lindbeck, 1990, p. 496)

I would look for "The New Ecumenism" to find its impetus among Christians from the Southern Hemisphere, among churches not currently aligned with the World Council of Churches, and with full participation from laity and clergy alike. I would expect them to take positions that are not currently in vogue among the ecumenical establishment. To the extent that they can develop more fully their ecumenical understandings as a community, they will succeed where current organizational attempts have failed. I would expect them, therefore, to call for greater emphasis on personal spiritual renewal and responsibility and to develop more sensitive understandings of what truly constitutes Christian community, but to be no less committed to work for peace, justice, and the environment.

Works Cited

Colson, Charles, and Richard John Neuhaus, eds. *Evangelicals and Catholics Together: Toward a Common Mission.* Dallas: Word, 1995.

Dayton, Donald. "Yet Another Layer of the Onion: Or Opening the Ecumenical Door to Let the Riffraff In," *The Ecumenical Review* 40, no. 1 (January 1988): 87-100.

Dulles, Avery. *The Craft of Theology: From Symbol to System.* New York: Crossroad, 1992.

Edwards, O. C. "The Far Horizon of Ecumenism: Roman Catholics, Evangelicals and Pentecostals as Potential Partners with the National Council of Churches," *Ecumenical Trends* 25, no. 2 (February 1996): 7-29.

Heim, S. Mark. "Montreal to Compostela: Pilgrimage in Ecumenical Winter," *The Christian Century,* 109 (April 1992): 333-35.

Heim, S. Mark. "The Next Ecumenical Movement," *The Christian Century* 112, no. 24 (14-21 August 1996): 780.

Lindbeck, George. "Confession and Community: An Israel-like View of the Church," *The Christian Century,* (May 9, 1990): 496.

Meeking, Basil, and John Stott, eds. *The Evangelical-Roman Catholic Dialogue on Mission 1977-1984: A Report.* Grand Rapids: Eerdmans, 1986.

Raiser, Konrad. *To Be the Church: Challenges and Hopes for a New Millennium.* Geneva: Risk Books/WCC Publications, 1997.

World Council of Churches. "Towards a Common Understanding and Vision of the World Council of Churches: A Policy Statement." Geneva: Central Committee, WCC, September 1997.

For Further Study

Cox, Harvey. *Fire From Heaven: The Rise of Pentecostal Spirituality and the Reshaping of Religion in the Twenty-First Century.* New York: Addison Wesley, 1995.

Gillquist, Peter, ed. *Coming Home: Why Protestant Clergy Are Becoming Orthodox.* Ben Lomond, CA: Conciliar Press, 1992.

Jacobsen, Douglas, and William Vance Trollinger, Jr. "Evangelical and Ecumenical: Reforming a Center," *The Christian Century* 111, no. 21 (July 13-20, 1994): 682-84.

Mouw, Richard. *Uncommon Decency: Christian Civility in an Uncivil World.* Downers Grove, IL: InterVarsity Press, 1992.

Webber, Robert E. *Evangelicals on the Canterbury Trail: Why Evangelicals Are Attracted to the Liturgical Church.* Waco, TX: Word, 1985.

V

CONFLICT, VIOLENCE,
AND MISSION

Introduction

The intention of these essays has been to deepen our grasp of the complex issues generated by this phenomenon called globalization, as well as to shed insights for local churches on their strategic role in this future. Never before in history will the manifestation by local churches of signs of the hope within them be so globally visible. God's call to congregations is to live as instruments of hope. Rather than blown over by the gale-force winds of global change, churches are to be empowered by the Spirit to chart the course toward the coming Kingdom. Central to this course is learning to live as peacemakers.

This final set of essays focuses on two pivotal forms of conflict in our global future — interreligious violence, and inter- as well as intranational war. What role does the church have in steering peoples away from these genocidal conflicts? Rather than fueling their incendiary destructiveness through prejudice and religiously sanctioned hatred, how can local churches be equipped to be instruments of peace?

John Witte first analyzes, and then offers practical guidance through two of the worst contemporary, interreligious battlefields: Orthodox-Evangelical conflicts, and those between Christians and Muslims. He approaches these by shedding insight on the different views of religious freedom held by Orthodox and by Muslims, than those of Evangelicals. Because Evangelicals tend to view freedom of religious choice not only

179

as an inalienable right, but also as a soteriological necessity, they've been unable to tolerate or even understand the seeming "intolerance" toward change within these other traditions. Witte provides insight into the rationale for these different notions of freedom. He also encourages a move toward greater humility among Evangelicals by providing reminders of the historic treatment of dissenters and those deemed to be heretics. Witte concludes by suggesting ways that all faith traditions may be encouraged toward greater religious tolerance.

Donald Shriver moves the discussion into the military and political realms. He chronicles ways in which religious people have both promoted, and less effectively, curbed our global propensity for violence. Each point he notes deserves extensive discussion and reflection within local churches. (Shriver provides more background in his book, on which this article is based.) With the increasing use of the military as peacekeeping forces, Shriver outlines ethical guidelines for the use of force to save life. The traditional "just war" guidelines don't provide adequate insight for response to our escalating intra-national conflicts. These ideas for turning military action into the pursuit of "humanitarian rescue" deserve debate and discussion by church groups. Never one to be accused of irrelevant meddling by a theologian, Shriver concludes by issuing two provocative challenges to American Christians.

Ian Douglas concludes this section by analyzing the implications of globalization for the missionary activity of local churches. With the escalating interest in "short-term" service by American Christians, he poses provocative questions regarding the motives, value, and outcome of this form of mission engagement. Our globalized communication, economic, and certainly transportation infrastructures provide more opportunity than ever before for travel and "cross-cultural" mission. Douglas notes that just as nation states are becoming less relevant in our global era, with communities and corporations establishing direct international relations that bypass governmental structures; so local churches are establishing direct mission relations that bypass denominational structures. However, will this enhance global community and understanding, or will it merely make more visible the alienating divide between the economic "haves and have-nots"? Is the American church's enthusiasm for mission a function of spiritual commitment or of personal affluence?

These three articles move our discussion of congregational mission beyond a debate over methods for numerical growth. They provide the basis for an urgently needed discussion within every local church regarding something as fundamental as what kind of world we want our children to inherit. What kind of global human community can we help create by the quality of our relationships with others? What steps can every congregation take to be an instrument of global hope and peace?

Tim Dearborn

13

Soul Wars

JOHN WITTE, JR.

A new war for souls has broken out in many parts of the world at the close of the second millennium. In some communities, such as the former Yugoslavia, local religious and ethnic rivals, previously kept at bay by a common oppressor, have converted their new liberties into licenses to renew ancient hostilities, with catastrophic results. In other communities, such as Sudan and Rwanda, ethnic nationalism and religious extremism have conspired to bring violent dislocation and death to hundreds of rival religious believers each year, and to persecution, false imprisonment, forced starvation, and savage abuses of thousands of others. In still other communities, most notably in America and Western Europe, political secularism and nationalism have combined to threaten a sort of civil denial and death to a number of believers, particularly "sects" and "cults" of high religious temperature or low cultural conformity.

The most heated new battles in this war for souls are between local and foreign Christian and Muslim groups in parts of Eastern Europe and Africa. With the political transformation of these regions in the past two decades, foreign religions gained new rights to enter these regions. In the 1980s and 1990s, they came in increasing numbers to preach their gospels, to offer their services, to convert new souls. Initially, local religious groups welcomed these foreigners. Today, they have come to resent these foreign religions, particularly those from North America and Western Europe who assume a democratic human rights ethic. Local religious groups resent the participation in the marketplace of religious ideas that democracy assumes. They resent the toxic waves of materialism and individualism that democracy inflicts. They resent the massive expansion of religious pluralism that democracy encourages. They resent the extravagant forms of religious speech, press, and assembly that democracy protects.

An increasingly acute war has thus broken out over the cultural and moral souls of these newly transformed societies and over adherents and adherence to competing forms of faith and ethnic identity. In part, this is a theological war — as rival religious communities have begun actively to defame and demonize each other and to gather themselves into ever more dogmatic and fundamentalist stands. The ecumenical spirit of the previous decades is giving way to sharp new forms of religious balkanization. In part, this is a legal war — as religious groups have begun to persuade local political leaders to adopt regulations restricting the constitutional rights of their religious rivals. Beneath a shiny constitutional veneer of religious rights and freedom for all, many East European and African countries have recently developed a legal culture of overt religious favoritism of some and oppression of others.

Two dimensions of this new war for souls will occupy us briefly here: (1) the struggle between Western and Eastern Christian understandings of mission, particularly those of Western Evangelicals and Orthodox believers in Russia; and (2) the struggle between Christian and Muslim understandings of the rights and rites of conversion. I shall first analyze briefly the theological and legal issues at stake in these two struggles, and then chart a few pathways for blunting some of the sharpest conflicts over them.

Orthodox-Evangelical Conflicts

At the heart of the political struggle between Western and Eastern Christians in Russia and other portions of Eastern Europe today are sharply competing theologies of mission. Some of these missiological differences reflect more general differences in theological emphasis. Eastern Orthodox tend to emphasize the altar over the pulpit, the liturgy over the homily, the mystery of faith over its rational disputation, the priestly office of the clergy over the devotional tasks of the laity. Western Christians generally reverse these priorities — and sometimes accuse the Orthodox of idolatry, introversion, and invasion of the believer's personal relationship with God.

These differences in theological emphasis are exacerbated by conflicting theologies of the nature and purpose of mission. Western Evangelicals, in particular, assume that, in order to be saved, every person must make a personal, conscious commitment to Christ — to be born again, to convert. Any person who has not been born again, or who once reborn now leads a nominal Christian life, is a legitimate object of evangelism — regardless of whether and where the person has been baptized. The principal means of reaching that person is through proclamation of the gospel, rational demonstration of its truth, and personal exemplification of its efficacy. Any region of the world that has not been open to the gospel is a legitimate "mission field" — regardless of whether the region might have another Christian church in place. Under this definition of mission, Russia and its people are prime targets for Evangelical witness.

The Russian Orthodox Church, too, believes that each person must come into a personal relationship with Christ in order to be saved. But such a relationship comes more through birth than rebirth, and more through regular sacramental living than a one-time conversion. A person who is born into the church has by definition started "theosis" — the process of becoming acceptable to God and ultimately coming into eternal communion with him. Through infant baptism, and later through the mass, the Eucharist, the icons, and other services of the church, a person slowly comes into fuller realization of this divine communion. Proclamation of the gospel is certainly an important means of aiding the process of theosis — and is especially effective in reaching those not born or baptized into the Russian Orthodox Church. But, for the Russian Orthodox, mission work is designed not to transmit rational truths, but to incorporate persons into communion with Christ and fellow believers.

This theology leads the Russian Orthodox Church to a quite different understanding of the proper venue and object of evangelism. The territory of Russia is hardly an open "mission field" which Evangelicals are free to harvest. To the contrary, much of the territory and population of Russia are under the spiritual protectorate of the Russian Orthodox Church. Any person who has been baptized into the Russian Orthodox Church is no longer a legitimate object of evangelism — regardless of whether that person leads only a nominal Christian life. Indeed, according to some Orthodox, any person who is born in the territory of Russia can at first be evangelized only by the Russian Orthodox Church. Only if that person actively spurns the Orthodox Church is he or she a legitimate target of the evangelism of others.

This is the theological source of the Russian Patriarch's repeated complaints about Western proselytism in Russia and other parts of the former Soviet bloc. The Patriarch is not only complaining about improper methods of evangelism — the bribery, blackmail, coercion, and material inducements used by some groups; the garish carnivals, billboards, and media blitzes used by others. The Patriarch is also complaining about the improper presence of missionaries — those who have come not to aid the Orthodox Church in its mission, but to compete with the Orthodox Church for its own souls on its own territory. The Patriarch takes seriously the statement of St. Paul, who wrote: "It is my ambition to bring the Gospel to places where the very name of Christ has not been heard, for I do not want to build on another man's foundation" (Rom 15:20).

International and constitutional human rights norms alone will ultimately do little to resolve this fundamental theological difference between Russian Orthodox and Western Evangelical and other Christians. "In seeking to limit the incursion of missionary activity we often are accused of violating the right to freedom of conscience and the restriction of individual rights," explained Patriarch Aleksii II. "But freedom does not mean general license. The truth of Christ which sets us free (John 8:32) also places upon us a great responsibility, to respect and preserve the freedom of others. However, the aggressive imposition by foreign missionaries of views and principles which come from a religious and cultural environment which is strange to us, is in fact a violation of both [our] religious and civil rights" (Aleksii, 1997, p. 103). The Russian Orthodox Church must be as free in the exercise of its missiology as Western Evangelicals wish to be. Both groups' rights, when fully exercised, will inevitably clash.

A theological resolution of this war for souls is thus as important as a human rights resolution. Interreligious dialogue, education, and cooperation sound like tried and tired remedies, but these are essential first steps. Self-imposed guidelines for prudential mission are essential steps as well. Foreign missionaries must know and appreciate Russian history, culture, and language; avoid Westernization of the gospel and First Amendmentization of politics; deal honestly and respectfully with theological and liturgical differences; respect and advocate the religious rights of all peoples; be Good Samaritans as well as good preachers; proclaim the gospel in word and deed. Such steps will slowly bring current antagonists beyond caricatures into a greater mutual understanding, and a greater Christian unity in diversity.

Western Christians, in particular, have much to learn from Orthodox worship — the passion of the liturgy, the pathos of the icons, the power of the silent inner spirit, the paths of pilgrimage of the soul toward God and his angels. Western Christian churches also have much to learn from Orthodox church life — the distinctive balancing between hierarchy and congregationalism through autocephaly; between uniform worship and liturgical freedom through use of the vernacular rites; between community and individuality through a trinitarian communalism, centered on the parish, the home, the babushka.

Orthodox Christians, in turn, have much to learn from their Western co-religionists — the emphasis on personal moral responsibility, stewardship, and vocation; the importance of daily devotion, regular penance, and individual spiritual growth; the cultivation of homiletics, Christian apologetics, and theological disputation; the insistence on the continued nurture and inherent plasticity of the Christian tradition.

The ultimate theological guide to resolve the deeper conflict over mission and conversion, however, must be a more careful balancing of the Great Commission and the Golden Rule. Christ called his followers to mission: "Go therefore and make disciples of all nations, baptizing them in the name of the Father and of the Son and of the Holy Ghost, teaching them to observe all that I have commanded you" (Mt 28:19-20). But Christ also called his followers to restraint and respect: "Do unto others, as you would have done unto you" (Mt 7:12). If both sides in the current war for souls would strive to hold these principles in better balance, their dogmatism might be tempered and their conflicts assuaged.

Christian-Muslim Conflicts

At the heart of a number of the conflicts between Christian and Muslim groups, not only in Eastern Europe but especially in Africa, is a fundamental controversy over the right to change one's religion, to convert. Most Western Christians believe in relatively easy conversion into and out of the faith. Most Muslims believe in easy conversion into the faith, but allow for no conversion out of it. Whose rites get rights?

International human rights instruments initially masked over these conflicts, despite the objections of some Muslim delegations. Article 18 of the 1948 Universal Declaration included an unequivocal guarantee: "Everyone has the right to freedom of thought, conscience, and religion; this right includes the right to change his religion or belief. . . ." Article 18 of the 1966 Covenant, whose preparation was more highly contested, became more tentative: "This right shall include to have or adopt a religion or belief of his choice. . . ." The 1981 Declaration repeated this same more tentative language, but the dispute over the right to conversion contributed greatly to the long delay in the production of this instrument. Today, the issue has become more divisive than ever.

"A page of history is worth a volume of logic," the great American jurist, Oliver Wendell Holmes, Jr., once said. And, on an intractable legal issue such as this, recollection might be more illuminating than ratiocination.

It is discomfiting, but enlightening, for Western Christians to remember that the right to enter and exit the religion of one's choice was born in the West only after centuries of cruel experience. To be sure, a number of the early Church Fathers considered the right to change religion as essential to the notion of liberty of conscience, and such sentiments have been repeated and glossed continuously until today. But in practice the Christian church largely ignored these sentiments for centuries. As the medieval church refined its rights structures in the twelfth and thirteenth centuries, it also routinized its religious discrimination, reserving its harshest sanctions for heretics. The communicant faithful enjoyed full rights. Jews and Muslims enjoyed fewer rights, but full rights if they converted to Christianity. Heretics — those who voluntarily chose to leave the faith — enjoyed still fewer rights, and had little opportunity to recover them even after full and voluntary confession.

Indeed, in the heyday of the Inquisition, heretics faced not only severe restrictions on their persons, properties, and professions, but sometimes unspeakably cruel forms of torture and punishment. Similarly, as the Lutheran, Calvinist, and Anglican churches routinized their establishments in the sixteenth and seventeenth centuries, they inflicted all manner of repressive civil and ecclesiastical censures on those who chose to deviate from established doctrine — savage torture and execution in a number of instances.

It was, in part, the recovery and elaboration of earlier patristic concepts of liberty of conscience as well as the slow expansion of new Protestant theologies of religious voluntarism that helped to end this practice. But, it was also the new possibilities created by the frontier and by the colony that helped to forge the Western understanding of the right to change religion. Rather than stay at home and fight for one's faith, it became easier for the dissenter to move away quietly to the frontier, or later to the colony, to be alone with his conscience and his co-religionists. Rather than tie the heretic to the rack or the stake, it became easier for the establishment to banish him quickly from the community with a strict order not to return.

Such pragmatic tempering of the treatment of heretics and dissenters eventually found theological and legal rationales. By the later sixteenth century, it became common in the West to read of the right, and the duty, of the religious dissenter to emigrate physically from the community whose faith he or she no longer shared. In the course of the next century, this right of physical emigration from a religious community was slowly transformed into a general right of voluntary exit from a religious faith, without encumbrance. Particularly American writers, many of whom had voluntarily left their Europeans faiths and territories to gain their freedom, embraced the right to leave — to change their faith, to abandon their blood, soil, and confession, to reestablish their lives, beliefs, and identities afresh — as a veritable *sine qua non* of religious freedom. This understanding of the right to choose and change religion — patristic, pragmatic, and Protestant in inspiration — has now become an almost universal feature of Western understandings of religious rights.

To tell this peculiar Western tale is not to resolve current legal conflicts over conversion that divide Muslims and Christians. But it is to suggest that even hard and hardened religious traditions can and do change over time, in part out of pragmatism, in part out of fresh appeals to ancient principles long forgotten. Even certain Shi'ite and Sunni communities today, that have been the sternest in their opposition to a right to conversion from the faith, do have resources in the Qur'an, in the early development of Shari'a, and in the more benign policies of other contemporary Muslim communities, to rethink their theological positions.

Moreover, the Western story suggests that there are halfway measures, at least in banishment and emigration, that help to blunt the worst tensions between a religious group's right to maintain its standards of entrance and exit and an individual's liberty of conscience to come and go. Not every heretic needs to be either executed or indulged. It is one thing for a religious tradition to insist on executing its charges of heresy, when a mature adult, fully aware of the consequences of his or her choice, voluntarily enters a faith, and then later seeks to leave. In that case group rights must trump individual rights — with the limitation that the religious group has no right to violate, or to solicit violation of, the life and limb of the wayward member. It is quite another thing for a religious tradition to press the same charges of heresy against someone who was born into, married into, or coerced into the faith and now, upon opportunity for mature reflection, voluntarily chooses to leave. In that case, individual rights trump group rights — with the limitation that the individual has no right to remain within the former religious community to foment reform or nonconformity therein.

Where a religious group exercises its trump by banishment or shunning and the apostate voluntarily chooses to return, he does so at his peril. He should find little protection in state law when subject to harsh religious sanctions — again, unless the religious group threatens or violates his life or limb. Where a religious individual exercises her trump by emigration, and the group chooses to pursue her, it does so at its peril. It should find little protection from state law when charged with tortious or criminal violations of the wayward former member.

There are numerous analogous tensions — generally with lower stakes — between the religious rights claims of a group and its individual members. These will become more acute as religion and human rights become more entangled in coming decades. Particularly volatile will be tensions over discrimination against women and children within religious groups; enforcement of traditional religious laws of marriage, family, and sexuality in defiance of state domestic laws; maintenance of religious property, contract, and inheritance norms that defy state private laws. On such issues, the current categorical formulations of both religious group rights and religious individual rights simply restate the problems, rather than resolve them. It will take new arguments from history and experience and new appeals to internal religious principles and practices, along the lines just illustrated, to blunt, if not resolve, these tensions.

Conclusion

Conventional accounts of law, human rights, and democracy often afford little space to religious ideas and institutions. Laws are often viewed as rules and statutes promulgated by the sovereign, not temporal elaborations of a divine or natural law. Human rights norms are viewed as secular claims to a good life, not complements to divine duties for right living. Democratic rulers are viewed as representatives of public opinion and vindicators of human rights, not vice-regents of God or champions of divine justice. To be sure, most writers today would agree that religious believers must be guaranteed liberty of conscience and free exercise of religion, and that religious institutions must be guaranteed collective worship and corporate organization. But religion, according to conventional accounts, is fundamentally a private matter with little constructive role to play in the drama of law, human rights, and democracy.

This conventional account takes too little account of the natural and necessary religious sources and dimensions of law, human rights, and democracy. Law, by its nature, is rooted in the ritual, traditions, and authority of religion, and draws in part on its ideas, institutions, and methods for its spirit and substance. Human rights norms are, by design, abstract statements of individual and associational living, which depend upon the religious visions of persons and communities to give them content and coherence. Democracy, by its nature, is a relative system of social organizations and political structures, which presupposes the existence of a body of beliefs and values that will constantly shape and reform it to the needs and ideals of the people. Religion is a natural and necessary source and dimension of any regime of law, democracy, and human rights.

It is undeniable that religion has been, and still is, a formidable force for both political good and political evil, that it has fostered both benevolence and belligerence, peace and pathos of untold dimensions. But the proper response to religious belligerence and pathos cannot be to deny that religion exists or to dismiss it to the private sphere and sanctuary. The proper response is to castigate the vices and to cultivate the virtues of religion, to confirm those religious teachings and practices that are most conducive to human rights, democracy, and the rule of law. T. S. Eliot once wrote, "Religions run wild must be tamed, for they cannot long be caged." Religion is an ineradicable condition of human lives and communities. Religion will invariably figure in the legal and political life of a community — however forcefully that society seeks to repress or deny its value or validity, however cogently the academy might logically bracket it from its political and legal calculus. Religion must be dealt with because it is perennially there, in various forms. It must be drawn into a constructive alliance with the regime of law, democracy, and human rights.

The regime of law, democracy, and human rights needs religion to survive. "Politicians at international forums may reiterate a thousand times that the basis of the new world order must be universal respect for human rights [and democracy]," Czech President Václav Havel declared in 1994 after receiving the Liberty Medal in Philadelphia. "But it will mean nothing as long as this imperative does not derive from the respect of the miracle of being, the miracle of the universe, the miracle of nature, the miracle of our own existence. Only someone who submits to the authority of the universal order and of creation, who values the right to be a part of it, and a participant in it, can genuinely value himself and his neighbors, and thus honor their rights as well" (Havel, 1994, p. 66).

Works Cited
Patriarch Aleksii II. *Pravoslavnaya Moskva* (March 1997), No. 7, p. 103.
Havel, Václav. Quoted in *Newsweek* (July 18, 1994), p. 66.

For Further Study

Nichols, Joel A. "Mission, Evangelism, and Proselytism in Christianity: Mainline Conceptions as Reflected in Church Documents," *Emory International Law Review* 12 (1998): 563-656.

Witte, John, and Johan D. van der Vyver, eds. *Religious Human Rights in Global Perspective*, 2 vols. The Hague/Boston/London: Martinus Nijhoff, 1996.

Witte, John, and Michael Burdeaux, eds. *Proselytism and Orthodoxy in Russia: The New War for Souls*. Maryknoll, NY: Orbis Books, 1999.

Witte, John, and Richard C. Martin, eds. *Sharing the Book: Religious Perspectives on the Rights and Wrongs of Mission*. Maryknoll, NY: Orbis Books, 1999.

14

The Taming of Mars:
Can We Help the Twenty-First Century
to Be Less Violent Than the Twentieth?

DONALD W. SHRIVER, JR.

Introduction

The date of October 28 will always have for me a set of memories mixed with love and dread. It happens to be the anniversary date of my parents' wedding in 1925. Sixty-seven years later, it became the birthday of our first grandchild, who is now aged six. In October 1962, the future father of that child, our youngest son, was not yet two years old. That month, our young family was traveling to my first post-Harvard job as a minister in Raleigh, North Carolina. On the way, we stopped by my parents' home in Norfolk, Virginia, arriving there in time to celebrate their anniversary.

All of this, of course, would be an ordinary insignificant item of personal family history except for one fact: The last weekend of October, 1962, was one of the most fearful weekends in all world history. It was the weekend we now call "the Cuban Missile Crisis," when nuclear-armed missiles, with their 900-mile range, were in reach of Norfolk, Virginia, site of the world's largest naval base. That weekend, the world was experiencing what we now know to have been our closest brush with the disaster of a nuclear war. It could have been the weekend that ended our child's chance to become a father and ours to become grandparents.

It will never be easy to *think* realistically and ethically about that or

193

any similar future catastrophe in world affairs. Did "mutually assured destruction" save us, these fifty years, from nuclear annihilation? If so, we have to say that the threat of potential great violence saved us from actual great violence. Was the risk always too great? Is it still so? If, as some say, we are not likely to have a "big war" anytime soon, has this fact simply opened up a new freedom for "little wars" all over the globe? At least fifty million humans perished in the violence of World War II, but in all the hundred years just past, humans have killed over a hundred and fifty million of each other. That is a world-historical record. Who can think of the twenty-first century without praying that its people will learn from the twentieth not to repeat its crimes?

Can Religion Help Contain Our Worldwide Propensity for Violence?

It's hardly a subject for humor, but when it comes to the question of whether religion "can" help solve any deep human problem, history is on the side of the answer that Dr. Maltby (of Scotland) gave to the parishioner who asked, "Can Christians dance?" Replied he: "Some can, some can't." Apparently some religions, and some religious people, can help diminish violence between humans. But equally apparent is the ability of religion, and some religious people, to *promote* violence. It is a very perplexing thing to think about, but one has to give religion a "plus" and a "minus" grade when the question of violence in history is up for consideration. On the minus side, one might summarize the power of religion for fortifying and empowering organized violence as follows. Religion and religious people have been least effective in curbing the organized violence of war:

- When its leaders have been so solidly allied with political leaders that the latter can easily assume that religious leaders will never disagree with their political decisions, including their decision to take their countries to war.
- When a theology of "two kingdoms" permits religious citizens to insulate "inside ethics" (e.g., inside the church) from "outside ethics" (i.e., ethics for secular society). This was the attitude of some Ger-

man Protestants in the 1930s regarding the actions of the Nazi state.

- When religious leaders raise questions about war so late in processes leading to war that there is little chance of their influencing those processes. Wars take time to stir up. Religion is sometimes too little and too late in protesting the coming of the war.
- When a customary desire for peace and harmony is so dominant in the thinking of a religious community that it has never given much attention to facing conflict and facing it without resort to violence. Conflict is a fact of life. Religious people often leave the field of conflict, letting it be dominated by others.
- When, while at war, the religious idea of the Devil begins to be applied to the enemy, who then begin to be classified as "inhuman, subhuman," and therefore easier to kill. Of all the contributions of religion to violence, this is perhaps the most vicious: as when a war is turned into a "Crusade," which happened when European Christians wearing the cross of Jesus went to war with Muslims.

But that is the dark side of the history. There is a brighter side. We can remember that religion has demonstrated some power to prevent deadly human conflict:

- When its leaders and members refuse to identify the cause of God with any political cause whatsoever and refuse to identify religious virtue with patriotism.
- When they have avoided an ethic that ignores politics and equally an ethic that "baptizes" politics.
- When, publicly and privately, they refuse to think of their country's enemies as "inhuman."
- When they draw on sources of information about the enemy — e.g., their missionaries — that counteracts some of the pictures of the enemy that a government finds useful for propaganda.
- When in public worship, they acknowledge that they, too, as citizens, are partly responsible for the oncoming evils of violence.
- When in their ability to *resist* in the name of God "the powers that be," they demonstrate the difference between nonviolent and violent resistance.

- When, as violent social conflict ends, they call for collective forms of repentance, restitution, forgiveness, and reconciliation on all sides, in ways that seek to prevent the repetition of such conflict in the future.

In our time, Christian churches have probably been at their best in this last kind of action. I think, for example, of the Marshall Plan after World War II, which sought to rebuild war-shattered Europe, a plan that the churches had much reason to support as over against the vengeance of the Versailles Treaty. And I think, too, of the postwar healing efforts of Church World Service, World Vision, and Catholic Relief. We seem, as Christians, to have some strong inclinations to pitch in and repair the damages left in the wake of war. But we have less confidence — and less power — when it comes to preventing war in the first place.

What contribution might religion and religious people make to preventing war? First, we can contribute by taking measures to control rampaging violence: We need to give more consistent attention to this question in our minds, in our prayers, and in our churches. We can also contribute by working toward a set of standards for humanitarian intervention in order to use force for the saving of life. And finally, we can acknowledge the need for our nation to abide both by the principles of international law and by the law of love laid down for us in Scripture.

Preventing Mass Violence: What Can Religion Do?

In the history of Christian thinking about war, there have been three major approaches. One is pacifism, affirmed by the early Christians as the only way of obedience to the teachings and the example of Jesus. The opposite second position, a thousand years later, was the Crusade, spiritually empowered violence. A third position, formulated by Augustine in the fifth century, was the idea of a just war, a view that has claimed the support of the majority of Christians down through history.

At its heart, the just war view answers a careful "yes" to the question: "Are there times when some violence is necessary for bringing greater violence to a halt?" The justification of police forces hangs on this "yes," and the existence of national guards and national armies.

There are just and unjust uses of these military organizations, says the theory: They are for defense, not aggression. They are not for destroying an enemy but for bringing the enemy's aggression to an end. They must discriminate between military and civilian targets. And they are to act in war in ways that prepare for peace, which means that they are to refrain from revenge and other acts that rouse a defeated enemy to want to go to war again

Reinhold Niebuhr expressed the spirit of the just war doctrine when he commented, "It may be possible for Christians to carry a gun in war, but they will carry it with a heavy heart." As a critic of the Vietnam War, Niebuhr showed that behind the "may be possible" and "heavy heart" was a refusal, on Christian grounds, to approve all wars. In this view, all wars are tragic. All are deep compromises to the love of God and neighbor. All are occasions for repentance on all sides.

My own Presbyterian Church (USA), in the summer of 1998, passed two resolutions that embodied something of this combination of resistance to the picking up of weapons and reluctant admission that there are sometimes ethical justifications for picking them up. The Assembly looked at the evidence that handguns kill more people (and especially children) in America than they protect, and it resolved 393 to 120 to ask every Presbyterian who had a handgun in his or her home to give it up.

The "right to bear arms" may or may not have been intended by the Constitution to apply to individual Americans, but the exercise of that right individually has helped to bring our country to the highest individual murder rate in the world. One control of violence, in most countries of the world, is the reserve of guns to a few authorized hands. A country — the U.S.A. — in which 200 million guns are in the hands of citizens is not a very safe country. It certainly proves unsafe for those fourteen American *children* who are killed by guns every day.

But to that resolution our Assembly added another longer, more complex resolution under the title, "Just Peacemaking." Behind this resolution was the insight that, by focusing on rules for a "just war," Christian thinkers have tended to divert attention from the rule that should (literally) be our Master-rule in this matter: "Blessed are the peacemakers, for they will be called the children of God" (Mt 5:9). In a time when war-making seems to continue unabated and, indeed, to be on the rise worldwide, are there arts of peacemaking to which the churches and Christian individuals are called to contribute? Is there even a way of thinking about the use of organized violence that may promise a diminishment of violence? In short, are there refinements needed in "just war" thinking that will shift emphasis from how a military force may make war justly to how it can justly make and keep peace?

The Use of Force to Save Rather Than to Destroy Life: Some Ethical Guidelines

The names Bosnia, Rwanda, Cambodia, and Kosovo call to mind the painful fact that mass murder has gone its rampaging way in many places in the past decade and the equally painful fact that international law and institutions are only beginning to cope with organized massacres. No one can claim to be an expert in this fearsome matter; but the time is overdue for citizens of all countries to ask what may be our common, global responsibility for protecting each other from these massive assaults on our lives.

There is a role, said a second 1998 Presbyterian resolution, for the use of military forces in a protective or "intervening" role. The resolution proposes these rules for turning military action in the direction of "humanitarian rescue":

1. It must respond to genuine human need, beginning with the need to preserve life.
2. When there is time, military intervention must be the "last resort" (like the just war theory), but lacking time and in face of sudden start-up of atrocity, it may have to be a first resort.
3. It should involve the least possible use of violence consistent with bringing peace — a rule of long standing in the just war tradition.
4. It should take place under international sponsorship, because the cause should be one that grows out of international law, a rule not present in the just war ethic.
5. It must "have a reasonable chance of alleviating the conditions it seeks to overcome," i.e., it must not simply add more increments of violence to an already violent situation.

198

6. It must not, in the name of "humanitarian" intervention, "cloak the pursuit of the economic or narrow security interests of the intervening powers." (For example, securing supplies of oil or advancing other trading interests are not the weighty provocation for intervention that is the prevention of mass murder.)
7. It must serve the general welfare of an entire population and not simply serve to increase the power of local or foreign leaders whose special interests may be under attack. (For example, a local war of peasants against large landowners cannot justly be settled merely by a forced restoration of the power of the landowners.)
8. It should seek to control, restrain, and perhaps to punish the leaders who organize the massacre. The great majority of mass murders in our time have been planned and effected politically. Leaders should be the chief targets of outside intervention and legal punishment.

Anyone who looks at these rules-for-humanitarian-intervention will know at once that they are difficult, incomplete, and open to improvement and debate by a broad cross-section of political leaders, military experts, and thoughtful citizens. In our new modern global connections, we seem to have more neighbors than we are comfortable even thinking about, which makes this subject a tough one for us all. The human community worldwide is still groping its way towards a time when it may actually *be* a human community. As we Christians struggle, like many others, for more light on the paths that lead us into the next century, however, there are two challenges that compel my attention. I want to conclude by commending them to the attention of other American Christians, too.

Conclusion:
Two Ongoing Challenges to American Christians

The first is the challenge of accepting the rights, the rules, and the responsibilities of *international law*. In the great 1776 Declaration, Thomas Jefferson wrote that as newly independent Americans we owe "decent respect to the opinions of mankind." These two hundred years later, we have seen impressive progress in international agreements on what those "opinions" are and ought to be. Among such agreements are the Universal Declaration of Human Rights, the Covenant of Economic and Social Rights, and other covenants (thanks to the catalytic work of the United Nations) against genocide, racism, environmental degradation, and violation of the rights of women. And now, beginning in 1998, a large company of nations has adopted a treaty for setting up an international court for the prosecution of leaders who perpetrate "war crimes and crimes against humanity."

Like all human law, these agreements are less than perfect; but they are an important advance over the notion that there are *no* rights and wrongs in the "jungle" of international relations, the idea that every nation is a law unto itself. Those of us who believe in one God, whose will we mean to obey "on earth as it is in heaven," can hardly believe that the idea of international law is impossible.

Unfortunately, however, many Americans apparently believe that our own nation has no need to be guided by an international law, because (they think) our laws are already superior to that of other countries and even to that of international bodies of which we are members. Is it not time to bring this belief into serious question? For example, is it likely that the behavior of a United States citizen on the world stage will *never* deserve the rebuke of an International Court? Almost two hundred years ago an American naval hero proposed a toast to his young nation: "To my country — may she ever be right, but right or wrong, my country!" It is not a toast that wise Christians in any country will ever propose. All do sin and "come short of the glory of God" (Rom 3:23); and all countries, too. In our churches, Christians should be consulting each other about this matter. In the long range there can be little international peace without international law.

There is a second challenge to us, related to the first. Obedience to law — beginning especially with the law, "Thou shalt not murder" — can be costly. In this brief space, I have tried to argue that at times the lives of some neighbors are worth the risk of the lives of others. That is the principle that has enabled many a soldier to believe that his or her calling is ethically noble. We know that the acts of only too many soldiers in human history have been anything but noble. Ideas of "Just Peacemaking" attempt to confine soldiering to the service of good causes and to exclude service in the cause of evil. But every war involves a mixture of good and evil, and the very idea of using violence to contain violence is logically as well as practically risky.

Nonetheless, there are times in the human community when great love for each other requires that we risk our lives for each other, and this possibility brings to Christians a challenging question: *Who* are the neighbors on whose behalf a Christian citizen of any country should consider risking his or her life? Were the warring tribes of Somalia worth the deaths of American soldiers? Could and should the deaths of 800,000 Rwandans have been prevented by strong, risky intervention of soldiers from other countries including the United States? Are we at a time in the history of the world when risking death for one's country is no longer the highest of causes, because there is a yet higher: risking one's life for the lives of neighbors anywhere on earth?

When Jesus answered the question, "Who is my neighbor?" (Lk 10:29) he seemed to have in mind just such a higher cause. It is time for us American Christians to consider the parable of the Good Samaritan in that light.

For Further Reading

Baille, Gil. *Violence Unveiled: Humanity at the Crossroads*. New York: Crossroads, 1995.

Huber, Wolfgang. *Violence: The Unrelenting Assault on Human Dignity*. Minneapolis: Fortress Press, 1996.

Shriver, Donald. *An Ethic for Enemies: Forgiveness in Politics*. New York: Oxford University Press, 1995.

Stassen, Glenn. *Just Peacemaking: Ten Practices for the Abolition of War*. Cleveland: Pilgrim Press, 1998.

Walzer, Michael. *Just and Unjust Wars*. New York: Basic Books, 1992.

15

Globalization and the Local Church

IAN T. DOUGLAS

I want to begin by saying that I probably would not have used the word "globalization" for I have found that "globalization" is not an unproblematic word. It has particular connotations that, in fact, I believe are contrary to the gospel of Jesus Christ. I have trouble reconciling the forces of globalization, in the secular world and the church, with the liberating power of the Spirit at the heart of the Pentecost movement. So, at the outset of this conversation, it is important to define terms, the nature of what we mean by globalization.

Globalization, loosely defined, is the act of making something global, worldwide, in scope and application. In the secular world, this process of making something worldwide often refers to the spread of economic and cultural realities generally associated with the capitalist, free-market forces of the industrialized West. The advent of transnational corporations, the exportation of music and video (MTV) to the far reaches of the world, and the incredible advances in communication and transportation, never imagined by our parents and grandparents, are representative of the forces of globalization.

Such globalization of the economic and cultural realities has both positive and negative effects. On one side the world's peoples have never been so closely connected and interdependent as we now are. Because of globalization, there is truly a global village in which the fluctuations of economic markets in Asia or financial difficulties in Russia have a direct impact on both the deal makers on Wall Street and the pensioner in middle America with a few dollars in a mutual fund. This web of economic interdependency shows that no one nation, no one economy, no one people is an island unto itself.

The globalization of economic and cultural realities, however, is also problematic. The growth and spread of a world culture and market economy have often come at the cost of local cultural and economic particularities. The result has been a growing homogeneity of society and a creeping cultural hegemony that discounts diversity and plurality of voices. The sociologist George Ritzer has described this homogenization process and loss of local cultural expressions as "the McDonaldization of society" (Ritzer, 1993). In the McDonaldized world, all people eat the same hamburgers and drink the same milkshakes, be they in Los Angeles, London, Moscow, or Beijing. In the McDonaldized world, those at the margins, those without power, suffer most, particularly indigenous peoples. It is they who lose their own ways of understanding God and the world, who lose their own means of production and sustenance. In the McDonaldized world the local, the vulnerable, the particular are always sacrificed to the interests and power of the global.

The church is not divorced from these processes of globalization. As this conference has recognized, the Christian community today is more global than it has ever been before. According to Anglican mission scholar David Barrett, at the beginning of the twentieth century 83 percent of the 522 million Christians in the world lived in Europe or North America. In the last four decades, however, we have witnessed the emergence of the church in Africa, Asia, Latin America, and the Pacific at the same time the church in Western Europe and North America has declined in power and numbers. As a result only 39 percent of the world's one and a half billion Christians live in the industrialized West (as of the year 2000). Barrett further predicts that by the year 2025, fully 70 percent of Christians will live in Asia, Africa, Latin America, and Oceania (Barrett, 1998).

How are we in the West to make sense of this radical change in the world Christian community? One way to describe the change is the "globalization of the church." The problem with such a view is that it presupposes a single unified expression of the church that is slowly encompassing the world. Like a transnational corporation with headquarters in Rome, Geneva, Canterbury, or New York, the "globalized" church seeks to set up subsidiaries in the Southern Hemisphere that are responsible to, or dependent on, the older "sending" churches of the industrialized West. Such a view of the global church leaves unchallenged the forces of cultural and economic hegemony upon which globalization theory is based. It presupposes that the churches of the Southern Hemisphere are offshoots of the Western church; younger, yes; economically poorer, probably; but still outposts of the sending churches.

An alternative view of the global Christian community would acknowledge that what God is about in the world today is a genuinely new thing and not simply an extension of the old. Many missiologists have attempted to describe the coming of the church in the Third World, or "two-thirds world," on its own terms. Such scholars have observed that throughout history the church has grown in one context as it has declined in another. Thus the First Church, the apostolic church of the Mediterranean and northern Africa, gave way to the Second Church of northern Europe and the industrialized West. Thus what we are witnessing today is not so much the globalization of a Euro-American church but the advent of a new church of the Southern Hemisphere, the Third Church. This Third Church is not a result of the globalization of Western churches but rather the ongoing movement of the spirit of God released at Pentecost. The younger churches of the Southern Hemisphere are related to the churches of the industrialized West but they are not an extension of them as globalization might suggest.

This panel is billed as: "Globalization and the Local Church." Having described some of the difficulties with the word "globalization," both in secular and ecclesial terms, let us now turn to the real focus of this morning's discussion, the local church. When I asked my friend Brian Sellers-Petersen what the planners had hoped this panel would be about, Brian described the increasing tendency of local congregations in the United States to eschew historic denominational structures and/or mission boards and engage in "mission" projects directly with churches in the Southern Hemisphere. I would suspect that we are all familiar with the phenomenon. A local congregation here in the United States makes a connection with Christians on the other side of the world through a variety of circumstances — a Tanzanian seminarian studying in the United States begins to worship in the parish, an elder traveling on business in Malaysia find his way into a church in Singapore one Sunday

204

morning, or a high school student learns about an Evangelical crusade in Buenos Aires while she surfs the Web. Before you know it there are real and tangible links established between the local parish in the United States and a Christian community in Tanzania, Malaysia, or Argentina. Letters and e-mails are exchanged; building projects are begun with funding from the United States; short-term mission trips for American youth groups are undertaken; doctors, teachers, and technical workers from the United States offer themselves for extended missionary service; and, on occasion, the church leader from Tanzania, Malaysia, or Argentina will travel to the United States, often exchanging pulpits with American pastors.

We must recognize that the local churches' ability to connect with other Christian communities around the world is, in and of itself, a manifestation of the realities of global communication and transportation. Like the globalization described above, this phenomenon of local American churches becoming, in one sense, their own mission agency has positive and negative ramifications.

On the positive side, the direct person-to-person linking that can be effected by the local parish reaching out to Christians on the other side of the world is to be celebrated. As Christians, we are people of the incarnation. We believe that God has been made known and accessible to us through God's real, live, flesh-and-blood presence in the world. The God who came to us in a humble stable, who walked among us and taught us on the road to Jerusalem, who died for us on a tree on Calvary and rolled away the boulder three days later, is every bit as real today as he was two millennia ago. As Christians we affirm that the body of Christ today, the church, continues that courageous incarnation in our own daily flesh-and-blood lives. Thus connecting, one to one, individual to individual, local church to local church, across the divides of culture, race, ethnicity, and geography, is a radical act of participation in God's ongoing incarnation. Thus local church direct participation in various mission projects throughout the global church allows for a new level of incarnational living. Today, more than ever before, individuals and local congregations have the opportunity, and responsibility, to reach out to other sisters and brothers in Christ around the world. As the old telephone commercial adage used to say: "Reach out and touch someone."

Or perhaps it might be better said: "Reach out and be touched by someone."

Like globalization itself, the possibility for local American congregations to connect directly with other Christian communities around the
world is not wholly unproblematic. From the mid-nineteenth century
up until the last few decades, most American mainline Protestant
churches supported denominational missionary agencies and/or mission boards. Generally speaking, the united mission board of a particular church served as a point of integration, unity, coordination, and national identity for local churches. In some cases the national mission
board and the denomination body were inextricably linked and functioned as a whole. Now it is true that these united mission boards
sometimes excluded those who might not have shared the dominant
missiological or theological position of the denominational agency. We
need to recognize also that women were often excluded because of their
gender from participation or leadership in the mission board, or at best
their presence was seen as "auxiliary." Even with these caveats, the
united missionary agencies and/or mission boards provided much of the
structures for American Protestant denominationalism. It was in the
common shared support of and participation in missionary outreach
that American mainline Protestants realized their shared identity as
Episcopalians, Congregationalists, Presbyterians, and Methodists.

Within the last three decades, the historic missionary agencies and
mission boards of American mainline Protestantism have come increasingly under attack. For a variety of religious, cultural, and economic reasons, the centralized denominational church structures that flourished
in the first part of the twentieth century have given way to downsized,
program-gutted, regulatory agencies. Long gone are the days of glory
when big church organizations provided common educational and missionary programs for their denomination, nationally and internationally. Local churches today are more likely to go it alone or find association with like-minded congregations outside their denomination than to
look to their denominational headquarters for guidance, networking,
and resources. What has resulted is a loss of denominational identity,
cooperation, and cohesion, and an increasing splintering of the American Protestant experience. One question before this panel then is: How
much has the increasing possibility for local churches to connect di-

rectly with Christian communities around the world contributed to the demise of American mainline Protestantism? How much have local church globalization successes come at the cost of national church programs and identity?

A corollary to the eschewing of denominational missionary agencies and mission boards in favor of local church initiative is the decline of conciliar missionary bodies and missiological imperatives. Since the World Missionary Conference of Edinburgh 1910, Christian churches around the world, at least of the more reformed traditions, have attempted to work together in the sharing of information and resources for mission. The successors to Edinburgh 1910, namely the International Missionary Council and the Commission on World Mission and Evangelism of the World Council of Churches, have always maintained that cooperation in mission is to be valued above independent action and isolated initiatives. The churches and mission boards associated with the IMC and the CWME of the WCC, specifically those of the Western industrialized nations, have learned over time what it means to be part of a genuine world Christian community. Such lessons in conciliar mission theology and engagement have come at great cost. I believe, however, that these lessons have served well both the ecumenical cause and the wider mission of God. The question thus needs to be asked: How much does local church involvement in global mission endeavors overlook the important ecumenical and missiological lessons of the last century of conciliar missionary cooperation? How much are local communities, in their rush to go it alone, bound to repeat the paternalist and colonial mistakes of past?

Finally, in our discussion we need to consider the economic realities of globalization and the local church. Which local churches are more likely to participate in mission ventures around the world? Is it not true that larger, richer congregations generally have more disposable income to spend beyond themselves than poorer, struggling churches? If this is so, then will the new face of American congregational involvement in the global church be primarily that of white, affluent Christians in a large, rich, suburban parish? Will mission be understood as the haves providing for the have-nots, economically speaking? What are the possibilities for mutuality and interdependence in such unequal relationships?

In these brief remarks, I have tried to trace the possibilities and difficulties of both the phenomenon of globalization as well as local church direct involvement in the world Christian community. It is clear that we are at a time of great transition in the church and in the world. I have thus tried to trace some of the complexities of this period in Christian history. I hope and pray that we will be able to live into our call "to restore all people to unity with God and each other in Christ."

Works Cited

Barrett, David B., and Todd M. Johnson. "Annual Statistical Table on Global Mission," *International Bulletin of Missionary Research* 22, no. 1 (January 1998): 26-27.

Ritzer, George. *The McDonaldization of Society: An Investigation into the Changing Character of Contemporary Social Life.* Thousand Oaks, CA: Pine Forge Press, 1993.

For Further Study

Buhlmann, Walbert. *The Coming of the Third Church.* Slough, England: St. Paul Publications, 1974.

Douglas, Ian T. *Fling Out the Banner: The National Church Ideal and the Foreign Mission of the Episcopal Church.* New York: Church Hymnal Corporation, 1996.

Dykstra, Craig, and James Hudnut-Beumler. "The National Organizational Structures of Protestant Denominations: An Invitation to a Conversation," in *The Organizational Revolution: Presbyterians and American Denominationalism,* edited by Milton J. Coalter, John M. Mulder, and Louis B. Weeks. Louisville: Westminster/John Knox Press, 1992. Dykstra and Hudnut-Beumler have used the regulatory agency metaphor to describe the current circumstances of the downsized centralized mission agencies.

Richey, Russell E. "Denominations and Denominationalism: An American Morphology," in *Reimagining Denominationalism: Interpretive Essays,* edited by Robert Bruce Mullin and Russell E. Richey. New York: Oxford University Press, 1994.

Walls, Andrew F. *The Missionary Movement in Christian History: Studies in the Transmission of Faith.* Maryknoll, NY: Orbis, 1996.

A Global Future for Local Churches

TIM DEARBORN

In the mystery of God's sovereignty, the One who is Lord of history and of nations has chosen to place local churches at the heart of the world's redemption. However, simple honesty dictates that we admit the obvious: the macrotrends that characterize our globalized future tend to leave local congregations breathless, appearing so small and insignificant. What possible impact can the average American congregation of fewer than two hundred members have on our post-industrialized, globally warmed, intra-nationalized, and fractured world? Surely the shapers of history are transnational corporations, as well as the few remaining nation states and regional tyrants. The "landmines" planted by previous generations in our soils, our environment, and our souls explode hope and leave people feeling like helpless victims.

At worst, many local American churches are, as Roland Robertson puts it, "globophobic" — terrified of our world. Many others are merely irrelevant — preoccupied with institutional survival and status. What seminary trains pastors to be global leaders? What church views its clergy as "global executives," charged with the responsibility to lead the flock into world-changing ventures? Some congregations do indeed charge boldly into the world, but may express the same missional triumphalism, and even paternalism, that characterized earlier days in the church's mission history.

God would indeed empower the church with a compelling vision for the twenty-first century. The God of the world's redemption has placed

209

the church firmly in the midst of the world. In fact, the church has never been more globally healthy, and never been better positioned for profound influence than it is now, at the beginning of a new millennium. Rather than being marginalized by the forces of globalization, sidelined in the sweep of massive change, local congregations face an unprecedented opportunity. God calls the church to ride the wave of global change, responding to the deep crises of human societies and human spirits created by that very globalization, with a breadth and creativity not found anywhere else. The twenty-first century will indeed be the century of the church — not the Church Militant or the Church Triumphant, but the Church Redeemed as a transnational, transcultural community of creative compassion.

For the church to respond most effectively to this rich opportunity, it must be prepared for tomorrow today! One aspect of that preparation is to be aware of some of the features of our global future, and how those features impact the life of local congregations. We are good at seeing the hand of God in history as recorded on the pages of Scripture. Yet we urgently need to see the hand of God in our contemporary world. What is God doing in our world? How is God calling the church to participate by the Spirit in this activity?

If we seek to see the "big picture" of our contemporary world and our immediate future, three macrotrends stand out as possible indicators of God's redemptive activity. Each has vital, but not necessarily obvious, implications for local churches. Each presents serious challenges and threats. Each also offers dynamic opportunities for local congregations in mission.

The Global Search for Community

Through the wonder of global communication, all of humankind can now see and even talk with one another. A World Cup soccer match can capture one-third of the world's eyes by satellite. Remote Himalayan villages in India can watch a live broadcast of the American Academy Awards. Internet chat rooms can connect people on five continents to discuss recent discoveries in science, or the care of their Tibetan terriers.

We can talk with one another, but we can't touch. Some assert that global communication is actually deepening our loneliness rather than our intimacy; it offers the semblance of community without the reality. The end of the twentieth century may well witness the triumph of individualism over community. Though more than half of humankind now lives in cities, in very intimate proximity to one another, we don't live in community. In fact, our cities themselves merely make our divisions more evident, and this trend will only intensify in the coming decades. In 1995, 2.1 billion people lived in cities; by 2025, the same number will live in urban slums with a total urban population of 4.9 billion. In other words, there will be as many urban dwellers in abject poverty in 2025 as there were people in cities in 1995. Roland Robertson describes globalization as the "compression of the world." This may lead to greater cohesiveness and integration. More likely it will lead to greater fragmentation.

The Global Search for Significance

Just as the late twentieth century evidenced the triumph of individualism over community, so there are signs of materialism's triumph over spirituality. The world has been turned into a global shopping mall, with the 7 M's (Michael Jordan, Michael Jackson, Madonna, Microsoft, McDonald's, m & m's, and Mickey Mouse) reigning as global cultural symbols. As never before, a large portion of world's population is informed by the same soap operas and news stories, and is dreaming the same dreams.

This global shopping mall is fueled by machines whose power far exceeds the meager influence of nation states (even so-called "superpowers"). Those engines are transnational corporations (TNCs). Fifty-one of the hundred largest economies in the world are TNCs, not countries. Only shareholders influence the dream makers of the world: governments don't control their ambitions and interests. The *Dreamworks* of the world are "elected" by dollars, not by votes.

Surprisingly, this global marketplace, filled with the same commodities sold by the same vendors, maintains an unexpected diversity. Roland Robertson refers to this as "glocalization," the particularization of global industries and trends. To increase their market share, corporate advertisers learn how to adapt their message and image to fit local niches, thus crafting the appearance of uniqueness. However, "glocalization" carries with it incendiary possibilities. Advertisers helping us dream the same dreams and nurture the same aspirations may invest millions of dollars, but the possibility of realizing those dreams is not equally shared. While global wealth increased by 40 percent in the 1990s, more than one billion people fell into even deeper poverty. In 1997, the combined income of the 447 wealthiest people in the world was greater than the combined income of 50 percent of the world's population. And now, thanks to global cities and global communication, those for whom the dream is unreachable know the addresses of those who are living the dream!

The Global Search for Security

The poor are watching how the rest live, and they are increasingly restless. The collapse of community, the confrontation with diversity, and rage over inaccessible possibilities drive people from despair to desperation. The lines of conflict are no longer as clear and simplistic as they were during the Cold War. Battle lines are now drawn between balkanized neighborhoods. We have already witnessed the incapacity of international organizations to bring intra-national order. The illustrations of this will only tragically increase in coming decades. Desperate people will resort to desperate measures like the bombing of the World Trade Center or other threats of terrorism. If trust has collapsed and all other options for survival have vanished, then one loses little by taking the path of violence.

The Global Ministry of Local Congregations

No wonder millions of people in the West are globophobic. No wonder escapist millennarial hopes are in the ascendancy and Y2K is viewed as an apocalyptic anagram. Yet such is not the biblical faith. Behind these macro trends we can see dynamic opportunities for local congregations.

In fact, we may be so bold as to say that we see the hand of God. Throughout history God has called the church to witness to the world of the wonder of life in Christ. For the first time in history, God has now brought the world to the church. Every local church is called to a global future. Local congregations will effectively exercise this global ministry and respond to the kairotic opportunity the Lord has set before them by demonstrating a transcultural community, a transeconomic significance, and a transnational security.

Transcultural Community

Local congregations are God's keys to community. Only in Christ can a path to unity be found that transcends ethnicity and economics, social status and class — without suppressing differences in a linguistic or social conformity. Only in Christ can diversity enhance unity — without furthering fragmentation. Behind the stirring in human hearts for greater community we can see the hand of God. These global cities are all beginning to look alike, whether they are in the West or the "two-thirds world." American cities are increasingly as multi-ethnic as two-thirds world cities. The Spirit of God is stirring local congregations to embrace the diverse world that God has brought to it, demonstrating the quality of community for which all humankind hungers. In fact, the church will have global credibility only to the extent that it has local diversity. World Vision has the privilege of witnessing this transethnic community, not only through our 12,000 staff from hundreds of cultural backgrounds, but also in the United States, where hundreds of local congregations are forming intimate bonds across ethnic divides through our CityLINC programs.

Transeconomic Significance

A second mark of local congregations as they live this global future is demonstrating to the world a new identity and sense of significance. In a world hungering for significance, local congregations once again have the opportunity to demonstrate a bold agenda. Rather than sharing our culture's addiction to the consumerist passion, naively assuming that through buying more our lives will be better, thousands of local congregations around the world are following the call of the Kingdom. As is often the case, our youth lead adults in pursuing this call. In 1998, 600,000 young people in America, and hundreds of thousands of others around the world joined hearts as they engaged in World Vision's *30-Hour Famine*. Through this commitment to fasting, prayer, service, and study about the causes of global hunger and poverty, these young people are embarking on a path of compassion that will lead them somewhere other than the shopping mall. As Richard Stearns, the president of World Vision, says:

> Poverty the issue is tremendously complex. Complex in its causes, its manifestations, and in its solutions. Poverty the issue is divisive, dividing haves from have nots, sometimes more powerfully than race, or ethnicity or religion. It causes broken relationships and it isolates the poor. It even causes division among those who seek to help. Poverty the issue often overwhelms us. It seems to mock our pitiful efforts. It makes even the most sincere of us cynical at times. It discourages, it stifles hope, and it fans the flames of despair. Poverty the issue defeats us, crushing our spirits much as it does the spirits of those that we seek to help. However, poverty, when we see it not as an issue but when we see it in the face of a person, is different. We can make a difference in the life of a person. We can in a relationship demonstrate the love of Christ in a tangible way. We can in a relationship overcome despair, rekindle hope, offer love.

God calls local congregations to nurture in one another the dream of the Kingdom, where all sorrows will cease and all injustices will end. This dream is lived out as we care for the poor in person, and not just in concept. This is our calling and our significance. Pursuing that Kingdom sets our feet on an adventure that is so challenging and dynamic that all so-called "virtual realities" seem dull and lifeless in comparison. Neither our youth nor our adults will want to waste time on a synthetic electronic replica of reality when the real thing is so captivating.

Transnational Security

Finally, behind the global incapacity to create durable sources of security we see the hand of God inviting local congregations to demonstrate a source of security that is rooted in time but extends into eternity. Only in Christ do we touch a hope that is so tangible that it takes all terror out of time and empowers us boldly to penetrate all darkness and despair. Local congregations are called to so root their members in this unshakable kingdom and utterly reliable hope that they manifest in the complexities of the present a redemptive alternative.

As Francis Fukuyama says, we are called to enable "the moral reconstruction of society by expanding the circles of trust" in our fearful societies. God invests congregations with social capital by endowing us with the ability to work together in spite of differences in ethnicity, income, and attitude. Congregations are thus empowered by the Spirit to serve with boldness in a fearful world.

Congregations have the profound calling and privilege to be local social glue. Actually, all glue, to be effective, must be applied locally — otherwise it paralyzes. The church will be most effectively global when it is indeed thoroughly local. God is stirring congregations to demonstrate the power of a community that transcends economics and ethnicity; that provides people with a significance more profound than mere consumerism; and that gifts people with such ultimate security, that they are released to live with bold abandon. Through this, members of our congregations will be set free to plunge into the chaos and pain that fills others' lives with the redeeming presence of God. As Francis Hesselbein proclaims, "the mission of God instills us with the passion and the patience for the long journey." Since this journey stretches all the way into the joy of eternity, its length is no longer problematic. We are free to persevere with joyous anticipation.

Thus, God calls church leaders to be global executives, equipping local churches for this global ministry. This call poses a great challenge for congregational leaders. According to a 1997 study by the Pew Charitable Trusts, only 23 percent of all Americans believe that improving the living standards of people in developing nations should be a high priority for U.S. foreign policy. In contrast, 72 percent of religious leaders place this as a high priority. Through a simple reading of Scripture, we are inescapably faced with the passionate priority God places on the poor. As Richard Stearns said, "The church in America misses out on much of God's blessing when it turns its back on the poor. When we turn inward to our own needs, focusing on sound systems, gymnasiums, musical programs, capital campaigns and even theological conferences, and we do it with a deaf ear to the cry of the poor, our churches will wither and find little blessing." The gospel enlarges our vision, our circle of trust and concern, and thus overcomes what Fukayama calls the "moral miniaturization of the world" — the shrinking of our sphere of concern. The gospel gives us "big hearts" and a moral vision for the kingdom of God penetrating our world's fragmented homes and societies.

Congregations of the twenty-first century will indeed be ones whose members are global citizens, with a loyalty and identity transcending ethnicity and nationality. These congregations will be the moral and relational glue binding our fractured globe. In this way, they will flood our troubled world with hope, as "the God of hope fills you with all joy and peace as you trust in him, so that you may overflow with hope by the power of the Holy Spirit" (Rom 15:13).

Contributors

David Befus is the Director of Micro-Credit at World Vision, International.

Susan Power Bratton is Associate Professor, Lindamar Chair/Biology Association, at Whitworth College.

Ron Cole-Turner is Professor of theology and science at Pittsburgh Theological Seminary.

Tim Dearborn is Dean of the Chapel and Associate Professor of Religion at Seattle Pacific University.

Ian Douglas is Associate Professor of World Mission and Global Christianity and Director of Anglican, Global, and Ecumenical studies, Episcopal Divinity School.

Kosuke Koyama is retired as the professor of World Christianity at Union Theological Seminary in New York.

John Mbiti is a representative to the World Council of Churches in Geneva, Switzerland.

Richard R. Osmer is the Thomas W. Synnott Associate Professor of Christian Education and Director of the School of Christian Education at Princeton Theological Seminary.

CONTRIBUTORS

James Ottley, Bishop of the Episcopal Church of Panama, was named the Anglican Observer to the United Nations by the Archbishop of Canterbury in 1994.

Scott Paeth is a Ph.D. student at Princeton Theological Seminary.

Cecil M. Robeck is the Director of the David duPlessis Center for Christian Spirituality and Professor of Church History and Ecumenics at Fuller Theological Seminary.

Lamin Sanneh is the D. Willis James Professor of Missions and World Christianity Professor of History, Yale University Divinity School.

William Schweiker is Associate Professor of Theological Ethics at the Divinity School, University of Chicago.

Donald Shriver is President Emeritus, Union Theological Seminary in New York.

Max Stackhouse is the Stephen Colwell Professor of Christian Ethics at Princeton Theological Seminary.

Mary Stewart Van Leeuwen is Director of the Center for Christian Women in Leadership at Eastern College in St. Davids, Pennsylvania.

Allen Verhey is Professor of Religion and Ethics at Hope College in Holland, Michigan.

John Witte is the Jonas Robitscher Professor of Law and Ethics, Emory Law School.